rage—all on the same page. The words she writes will matter to you. They will change the way you see—everything. Kenny's courage to say the things that need to be said is only matched by the skill with which she wields her proverbial pen. All hail this new and necessary voice."

—**Lisa Sharon Harper**, author of *The Very Good Gospel* and *Fortune: How Race Broke My Family and the World—and How to Repair It All*

"By times wise and tender, then grab-you-by-the-lapels prophetic truth-telling, Kenny's passion, anger, and hope for disability justice is utterly embodied. I found this book to be not only a call to justice but an invitation to deep blessing. I will be pressing this book into the hands of every ministry leader I know."

—**Sarah Bessey**, editor of the *New York Times* bestseller *A Rhythm of Prayer* and author of *Jesus Feminist*

"Kenny describes with wit and candor her experiences as a disabled Christian in worship services and Bible studies, but also in places like the DMV, high school, the doctor's office, and Disneyland—showing, lamentably, how ableism at church looks just like it does everywhere else. She raises up the way of Jesus to practice holistic healing in the face of ableism's holistic harms. Kenny issues a convicting invitation to the people of God to live up to our deepest values and to stop excluding the necessary gifts of our disabled kindred, for the good of all. I will be giving this book to my disabled and nondisabled friends alike."

—**Bethany McKinney Fox**, author of *Disability and the Way of Jesus: Holistic Healing in the Gospels and the Church*

"In Kenny's outstanding debut, she tells us this book is her unstifled scream. Are we listening? I am screaming alongside her when I read about how we as the church harm her and other disabled people. Kenny exegetes not only Scripture and individuals with precision but also the American system and the church. Our theology and our actions demonstrate that many are anything but pro-life—we are guilty of ableism and eugenics, and we need to repent. Kenny is among the sharpest writers and thinkers, and she offers the truth through beautiful writing, wit, wisdom, and grace while showing us the way forward."

—**Marlena Graves**, author of *The Way Up Is Down: Becoming Yourself by Forgetting Yourself*

"Incisive, witty, and revelatory, *My Body Is Not a Prayer Request* is a much-needed prophetic intervention against the ableist 'common sense' that prevails in many churches. This work is sure to be a balm for those who have ever felt sidelined because of ableist theology and sure to be a redemptive kick in the pants for the rest of us."

—**Andre Henry**, award-winning singer-songwriter, writer, and activist

MY BODY IS NOT A PRAYER REQUEST

Disability Justice in the Church

AMY KENNY

Brazos Press
a division of Baker Publishing Group
Grand Rapids, Michigan

Published by Brazos Press
a division of Baker Publishing Group
PO Box 6287, Grand Rapids, MI 49516-6287
www.brazospress.com

Printed in the United States of America

Library of Congress Cataloging-in-Publication Data
Names: Kenny, Amy, 1987– author.
Title: My body is not a prayer request : disability justice in the church / Amy Kenny.
Description: Grand Rapids, Michigan : Brazos Press, a division of Baker Publishing
    Group, [2022] | Includes bibliographical references.
Identifiers: LCCN 2021050092 | ISBN 9781587435454 (paperback) | ISBN
    9781587435669 (casebound) | ISBN 9781493437092 (ebook) | ISBN
    9781493437108 (pdf)
Subjects: LCSH: People with disabilities—Religious life. | Church work with people
    with disabilities.
Classification: LCC BV4910 .K46 2022 | DDC 248.8/61—dc23/eng/20211130
LC record available at https://lccn.loc.gov/2021050092

Baker Publishing Group publications use paper produced from sustainable forestry practices and post-consumer waste whenever possible.

23   24   25   26   27   28   8   7   6   5   4

For every disabled person
wondering whether you fit in,
fretting that you are too much.
You, with your canes, crutches,
chemical sensitivities, and CART,
are worthy of belonging.

You are enough.

Contents

A Note on Language

Much ink has been spilled on whether we should use people-first language ("people with disabilities") or identity-first language ("disabled people") when talking about disability. I respect the various ways disabled people wish to be identified. Throughout the book, I use "disabled people." For me, choosing this moniker is a way of shunning the shame often associated with disability and proclaiming that "disability" is not a bad word. I am not a euphemism or a metaphor. I am disabled.

Preface

I was in the hospital when my nephew was born. Not in the labor and delivery ward but in the cardiology department, thirty miles away. "It's probably nothing," they reassured me. "We just want to rule out any heart complications." Probably nothing. I mulled over how many hours of my life and dollars on my credit card were devoted to probably nothings.

Before I learned the name of my disability, I was informed it was probably nothing. When my appendix burst, I was assured it was probably nothing. Before my ovarian surgery, I was pacified by doctors that it was probably nothing.

"Probably nothing" was becoming the story of my life.

I downloaded a picture of my nephew on my phone as I waited. His face looked serene. My brother's texts brimmed with exclamation points: "He's here!" I wondered at the joys a hospital can bring, in a different department and a different life, where being "here" is where you want to be and not what you dread. There was no excitement to be found in the "here" of my overly refrigerated room with linoleum floors, vinyl chairs, and cliché art that pretends someone cares. While waiting for my probably nothing, I tried to distract myself by reading an article on my phone about the impending cicada summer.

These insects, which look like a cricket, a moth, and a fly had a baby with a beetle, lurk underground for seventeen years before rising up and screaming. Imagine witnessing our world for the first time when you are seventeen, only to find it so lacking that all you can do is scream. Of course, the male cicadas are the ones who screech. (We'd likely brand the female cicadas "too emotional" if they screamed.) Cicadas can't make noise with their mouths, so they pull their abdominal membranes (called tymbals) together so quickly it produces a clicking sound that rivals the decibels of a chain saw or a lawn mower.[1] Their mute mouths don't stop these disabled bugs from making themselves heard. Even the cicadas cry out!

There under the florescent light, learning about these belting bugs, my body was already screaming. The contracting muscles of my chest reverberating in my ears. Jolts of my nervous system erupted like fireworks. If only someone would listen.

I left the hospital uncertain, wearing my heart—at least, the printout of my heart's rhythmic music—on my sleeve. It flapped in the wind as I made my way to the car, my cane not the type of support I needed. How can a machine measure a broken heart? Where does the pain go on the printout, in between the valleys of the shadow of death?

It turned out it wasn't a broken heart, at least not the medical kind. It was a broken nervous system. "General dysfunction" is the phrase the white coats used. My muffled scream pounded inside my chest as I longed for an explanation for my body outside the space between "probably nothing" and "general dysfunction."

1. For more on cicadas, check out the article I read in the hospital: Janet Loehrke and Doyle Rice, "Cicadas Have Emerged in 2021: A Visual Guide on How Loud Will They Get and How Long They Will Be Around," *USA Today*, March 30, 2021, https://www.usatoday.com/in-depth/graphics/2021/03/30/a-visual-guide-to-2021-cicadas/4670176001.

The worst of it wasn't the hospital tests or even the doctors' cavalier words. It was the way I had stifled my own screams. For so long I have kept my pain hidden, underground, so it cannot be dismissed by anyone. Smiling instead of wincing, reporting that I am "fine" instead of divulging the truth of the torture, shielding people from the ache of disability slurs, dreading that my wounds will scare people off.

But some days, I just want to scream. My body wants to scream out so loudly that no one can deny it, in decibels louder than a lawn mower. I have waited longer than seventeen years for my screaming summer, when everyone listens to my disabled body shriek.

This book is my scream. On its pages you might find parts of my story that make you feel uncomfortable, confused, or even convicted. I hope that you continue reading, knowing that these moments of discomfort are points of departure rather than destinations. Just like the noise of my disabled cicada friends, my screams are a call to action. A call for the church to value disabled people as image-bearers and learn from the prophetic witness of our numerous gifts.

As you listen to my screams, may they call you to join me in reimagining the church together. May they reverberate until no disabled person ever has to stifle their screams again.

Disability Curatives

"God told me to pray for you," she says. Her words linger like cloying perfume in a claustrophobic space. "God wants to heal you!" She is undoubtedly thrilled with this opportunity.

I've been here before. It never ends well.

This woman does not know me. She doesn't have the intimacy that prayer or accountability or sarcasm require. She simply interprets my cane as something that requires "fixing" and ropes God into her ableism, the belief that disabled people are less valuable or less human than our nondisabled counterparts.[1] Internally, I make a swift calculation: endure the prayer to avoid squabble, or call her out on her benevolent eugenics and be branded a heretic again.

I used to play the game. Eavesdropping as they prayed for my broken body, trying to conceal my spasms lest they be confused for demonic convulsions. I thought if I could just assume a veneer of piety, it would inoculate me against their

---

1. For a broader definition of ableism, check out the working definition by Talila A. Lewis: "Ableism 2020: An Updated Definition," January 25, 2020, https://www.talila lewis.com/blog/ableism-2020-an-updated-definition.

patronizing prayers and invasive interrogations. I believed that I could perfect my way out of people demeaning disability, that somehow my patience would endow me with enough worth in their minds to be considered fully human. All it did was put me on a carousel of dehumanization that made me feel complicit in their toxic theology.

So I choose door B. "I don't need prayer for healing. My body has already been sanctified and redeemed," I choke out. I know it won't be enough, but my dignity is not up for debate, particularly here, in God's house. Only a second has passed, but there is a lifetime between us.

Bewildered, she blocks my path, grabbing my forearm so I can't leave until I suffer her pontification. "You *need* to hear that God wants to heal you. If you stopped resisting, you would be free already." Free. All I want to be free from is *her*. All I need to be liberated from is the notion that disability is inherently deviant and in need of eradication.

I am the embodiment of her worst-case scenario because I don't need her to rescue me. I am what every athlete fears and what pregnant parents dread. I am the catalyst for losing faith and questioning God. Theodicy runs through my veins. I am every villain in every superhero movie ever made. People call my murderers "merciful" because I am a burden and a drain and a waste. I am disabled.

This woman is an echo of every prayerful perpetrator before her. They have many faces, but they always approach me with the same paternalistic confidence, eager to rid me of my wheelchair or cane. On repeat, they applaud the stories where Jesus healed a disabled outcast like me, without stopping to consider that curing bodies and healing lives are not the same thing. They are too hyped up on their divine intervention to realize they are not the savior in my story. A poor, brown-skinned refugee named Jesus is.

Flummoxed, the woman snaps that I have given up, that God wants more for me than life in a wheelchair. That Jesus's divine touch is waiting whenever I am willing to receive. The mark of her nails dissipates long before her words do.

They think they are being faithful; that much I want to believe. But some days it is hard to convince myself of their pure intentions because I am the only one who emerges singed by these encounters. This woman uses the prayer card to justify imposing her prejudice on a stranger she assumes despises being disabled. I am not *confined* to my wheelchair. I have not *lost* a battle to a disease. I am many things, but a tragic defeat is not one of them.

Afterward I replay the encounter in my mind, wondering what I should have said differently, knowing there will be a next time. I wish I was whole in their minds—enough to exist without needing a prayerful remedy to cast out my "demons," a full human who has something to offer other than a miraculous narrative. I wish I could be more than my diagnosis, more than a problem in need of fixing, as if my disability is only valuable if converted into a cure. I wish prayerful perpetrators were free from the lie that I am worth less simply because my body works differently. In each of these encounters, I come away feeling like my stomach has just dropped out on a roller coaster. I am confused by the way people interpret my disability as in need of "fixing" without knowing anything else about me. I am troubled that my body becomes public property they feel they have the right to control. I am indignant that this takes place under the veil of Jesus-following, as though they are the bouncers to God's table. I am hurt that I must justify my own existence at church. Belonging shouldn't have the admission price of assimilation.

My story is not unique. Most of my disabled friends have their own stories of strangers approaching them to pray away their disabilities, sometimes at church, other times on public transport or at the grocery store. No place is safe from prayerful perpetrators. It's draining to endure, especially because the people who do this don't intend to cause us harm. They just haven't considered how the assumption that disability needs "fixing" is dehumanizing.

Some of the irony is that my life isn't disastrous or deficient at all. Most days, my disability isn't the worst part of my day, or even what I need prayer for. To assume that my disability needs to be erased in order for me to live an abundant life is disturbing not only because of what it says about me but also because of what it reveals about people's notions of God. I bear the image of the Alpha and the Omega. My disabled body is a temple for the Holy Spirit. I have the mind of Christ. There's no caveat to those promises. I don't have a junior holy spirit because I am disabled. To suggest that I am anything less than sanctified and redeemed is to suppress the image of God in my disabled body and to limit how God is already at work through my life. Maybe we need to be freed not from disability but from the notion that it limits my ability to showcase God's radiance to the church. What we need to be freed from is ableism.

"If your hand causes you to sin, cut it off. It is better for you to enter life crippled than with two hands to go to hell, to the unquenchable fire. And if your foot causes you to sin, cut it off. It is better for you to enter life lame than with two feet to be thrown into hell. And if your eye causes you to sin, tear it out" (Mark 9:43–47 ESV). We get it, Jesus. It's better to be lame, blind, and crippled than go to hell. It feels a little extreme to perform voluntary amputations to avoid sin. We'd have a lot more folks with amputations in our midst if we took this literally. Yet Jesus still claims that disability becomes a way to encounter God or a preventative remedy for sin, suggesting that being nondisabled might enhance temptation. I am not trying to initiate a #CutItOff movement, but I wish the church could interpret my disabled body in this way: as a mark of holy living, an antidote to sin, and a way to reveal God to the surrounding community. Churchgoers have been too hasty to dismiss passages of Scripture where disability is celebrated as a blessing or a prophetic witness, because it doesn't fit their neat cultural narrative of disability making people uncomfortable. Imagine if prayerful perpetrators #CutItOff instead of trying to pray me away.

This isn't the only time Jesus talks about disability as a teacher and a way to reveal God to nondisabled people. When Jesus encountered a man born blind in Jerusalem, "his disciples asked him, 'Rabbi, who sinned, this man or his parents, that he was born blind?' Jesus answered, 'Neither this man nor his parents sinned; he was born blind so that God's works might be revealed in him'" (John 9:2–3). Just like the prayerful perpetrators who approach my wheelchair with head tilts and side-glances, the disciples interpret this man solely as his disability. They are so caught up in prescribing the cause of his disability that we don't even learn his name. Do they even know it, I wonder? He's known as the man formerly known as blind, which sounds like a dad joke about Prince. I hate that he is not given a name, as though he is unknown and forgotten, not important enough to name. I know what it's like to be reduced to a diagnosis, and I want this man to be given more humanity and dignity than that. So let's call him Zechariah, which means "God remembers." Zach is so much more than his blindness. "I am the man," he confidently enlightens his neighbors, wanting them to know who he really is, in addition to his disability (v. 9). We also get a sense of his personality throughout the chapter: he's not afraid to challenge authority figures, and he's feisty. He seems like someone who would use the eye-roll and face-palm emojis with regularity. (Who doesn't?) Zach advocates for himself when confronted by his neighbors because he knows who he really is. Perhaps the disciples never initiated a conversation with him because in their minds, Zach's identity *is* his blindness—a blindness that they incorrectly conflate with sin.

It's easy to dismiss the disciples as the villains here, but they surely think they are being faithful to common theology inherited from Leviticus. They aren't excluding Zach for the sake of excluding, like *Mean Girls*, but want to remain faithful to their notions of who is in and who is out. In their minds, it's much simpler if there's a neat conflation of sin and disability. Much like prayerful perpetrators, the disciples understand the disabled body as public property they can control, interpret, and reject. No disabled person can sit with them.

Before you judge the disciples, you should know that a 2018 poll found that 67 percent of people feel "uncomfortable" *talking* to a disabled person.[2] Disabled people make up about 25 percent of the US population, and 15 percent of the global population, yet we still make the majority of our neighbors uncomfortable, simply by existing.[3] Any body who doesn't fit in a tidy box of cured or "normal" makes other people feel out of place. It is no wonder the disciples don't know anything about Zach other than his blindness. They don't bother to get involved in his life because they think they are better than him.

Jesus is having none of it. Jesus inverts their idea of blindness by showing the disciples that disability becomes a place of encounter with the glory of God. Jesus interacts with Zach directly, talking not just *about* him, but to him and with him. According to Jesus, Zach's blindness didn't result from his or his parents' sin, but instead his blindness displays God. What a powerful, subversive statement: disability helps reveal the Light

2. This statistic is according to the Scope report about attitudes and equality for disabled people: Simon Dixon, Ceri Smith, and Anel Touchet, "The Disability Perception Gap: Policy Report," Scope, May 2018, https://www.scope.org.uk/scope/media/files/campaigns/disability-perception-gap-report.pdf.

3. For more statistics related to disability in the US population, check out Disability and Health Data System from the Centers for Disease Control and Prevention, http://dhds.cdc.gov.

of the World to people who think of themselves as holier than disabled people. Disability is no longer a symbol of sin but one of being open to revelation. Disability unveils God's work to the community, if only people are willing to receive it.

Jesus returns to this messaging later, claiming that he's come to the world "so that those who do not see may see, and those who do see may become blind" (John 9:39). While this is directed at Jesus's audience, it offers a lesson for modern Jesus followers. If our primary perception of ourselves is as people who can see, hear, or walk—over those who can't do those things—the sin of stereotyping and excluding remains prevalent. According to Jesus, those who think of themselves as "able-bodied" may be in more need of healing than those who are disabled. "But that's figurative," you're tempted to clap back. Paul, blinded on the road to Damascus, begs to differ. Figurative or not, the fact that a disabled person makes two-thirds of us uncomfortable exposes the need for deeper healing. Instead of dismissing these statements as merely figurative, we should consider how to embrace disability as a mark of greater understanding about God. Disability acts as a method for revealing the living God to the community, not something that always needs to be prayed away to showcase God's power. Imagine if the prayerful perpetrator approached my wheelchair with reverence and awe instead of condemnation and accusation. Maybe then they would be able to witness the glory of God revealed through my disabled body.

Perhaps the biggest surprise in this passage is that receiving sight doesn't magically improve everything (or anything?) for Zach. Quite the opposite, in fact. It amplifies the way he is ostracized by people who think they understand Scripture better than him. His neighbors fancy themselves detectives on *Law & Order: Jerusalem*, interrogating everyone to get to the truth of how and why and when he was first able to see. "They reviled him, saying, 'You are his disciple, but we are disciples of Moses. We know that God has spoken to Moses, but as for this man, we do not know where he comes from. . . . You were born entirely in sins, and are you trying to teach *us*?' And they drove him out" (John 9:28–29, 34). The neighbors are so suspicious of Zach's miraculous story that they expel him, baptizing their actions in spiritual language to make them seem holy. Zach receives his sight on the Sabbath, which breaks the rules, and that matters to them above all else. "Make it make sense!" the neighbors seem to whine. But they don't stop at curiosity or even confusion; they go straight for expulsion. The neighbors are every prayerful perpetrator, demanding answers to questions I am not asking ("Why are you disabled?" "What unconfessed sin is preventing you from getting up and walking?"); challenging me to ace their faith litmus tests; dismissing my body because of the fall. Religious neighbors then, as now, want disability to stop making them uncomfortable. Insert God here to make ableism seem holy.

Sermons on John 9 love to zoom in on the miracle and act as if nothing else in the chapter matters. So long as we don't have to talk about disability, it's all good. But the passage itself doesn't read this way. Almost all of the chapter focuses on what happens *after* Zach receives sight. If it were just about the physical cure, the story would end after verse 7 when he reemerges from the pool, able to see. Yet the chapter continues for another thirty-five verses, focusing on how the neighbors retort and deport Zach. Jesus doesn't even stick around to witness the results of this swim; he doesn't come back until after the municipal interrogations. Structurally, the focus is not on the physical but on something deeper and richer that Jesus offers to Zach. It is true that Jesus cured people's bodies as part of his ministry, but this passage is often misinterpreted to perpetuate the notion that disabled people require physical modification to be complete.[4]

---

4. I realize that our modern notion of disability is not the same as the notion common in antiquity. For more on this nuance, check out Amos Yong, *Theology and Down Syndrome: Reimagining Disability in Late Modernity* (Waco: Baylor University Press, 2017).

Jesus's ministry is not all about a physical cure but about holistic healing.

Today, we typically think of illness (and sometimes disability) as biological, with Western medicine set up to find and cure disease directly. When Westerners go to the doctor, it's usually to find a cure for whatever symptoms we're experiencing. I'm in pain: fix it, medicine. Folks in Jesus's day thought about healing in much broader terms. They talked about healing as restoring relationships and integrating someone back into social and religious systems.[5] The Greek word often used in Scripture for healing is *sozo*, which means "to make whole" or "to save."[6] It's the same word used to talk about salvation. Jesus's healing is not purely about a physical alteration but about reestablishing right relationship between humanity and God and, hopefully, between individuals and community.[7] Healing allows people to flourish. Modern medicine still recognizes the difference between curing and healing. Curing is a physical process; it's individual, usually (fairly) rapid, and concentrates on eliminating disease. Healing is a sociocultural process. It focuses on restoring interpersonal, social, and spiritual dimensions. It's lengthy and ongoing because it's a process of becoming whole.

The difference might best be understood in trauma cases. If a soldier is shot, the bullet wounds can be sewn up, and infection from any lingering shrapnel can be treated with antibiotics. That's curing. It resets the body to its physical state *before* the trauma occurred. But true healing might not occur until much later, when the soldier has processed the event and waded through the emotional labor of the aftermath. Healing

5. Bethany McKinney Fox, *Disability and the Way of Jesus: Holistic Healing in the Gospels and the Church* (Downers Grove, IL: IVP Academic, 2019), 15–25.

6. John Wilkinson, *The Bible and Healing: A Medical and Theological Commentary* (Grand Rapids: Eerdmans, 1998), 5.

7. *The Jewish Annotated New Testament*, edited by Amy-Jill Levine and Marc Zvi Brettler (Oxford: Oxford University Press, 2011), uses different words for "curing" and "healing" throughout the translation as well.

is nonlinear. It takes time. One day you feel brighter, so you get out of bed. The next, you can't lift your neck without slumping back on the pillow, like the air escaping from a balloon. The goal of healing isn't fixing, but restoring. It's a transformative process that seeks to make someone whole. Healing is not about erasing the experience of trauma (which I'm pretty sure is impossible) but about processing it and coming to terms with it, no matter how heavy it might be to carry.

Zach received a physical cure in the beginning of John 9 when he emerged from the pool able to see, but his true healing does not occur until much later in the chapter, when he declares, "Lord, I believe," and worships Jesus (9:38). That's the moment he's restored through a conversation with the living God and is finally able to reach the place of worship he's been excluded from. Jesus is always tearing down the boundaries we put up, and here Jesus reveals the unnecessary barriers of kingdom exclusion. Everyone is now welcome at the table! Zach can worship Jesus anywhere, even outside the temple, even on the Sabbath, even without the permission of the religious elite. That's the moment he realizes who Jesus truly is: not some random magician or prophet, but the Son of Man. *That's* when he's healed.

In the disability community, disability is often described as a social construct.[8] This means people are not disabled because of bodily differences but because of systemic barriers in a society

---

8. For more on the different models of disability, check out Angi English, "The Social Construction of Disability," *Medium*, July 30, 2014, https://medium.com/homeland-security/the-social-construction-of-disability-999114247359. This is just one model of disability; all models are incomplete, since disability is a broad constellation of embodiments and experiences. Each model has something to teach us about the disability experience.

built around nondisabled people. Those barriers include inaccessible buildings, hiring discrimination, paying disabled people sub–minimum wage (still legal in the US!), and a general attitude of belittling anything perceived as difference.[9] A similar construct of disability occurs in some Indigenous cultures, which define disability "in relational rather than bodily terms. . . . Though individuals might experience impairment, disability would come only if or when a person was removed from or was unable to participate in community reciprocity."[10] This is not to suggest there are not medical issues connected to disabled embodiments. Disability encompasses a broad constellation of bodies, minds, and experiences, so the social construct cannot account for everyone, but it is a helpful framework for naming how the structures we have put in place often disable people more than individual bodies do.

Not all disabled people are in pain. (I am because I'm just lucky like that.) Not all suffer from our bodies, but *all* of us suffer from the way society mocks or limits those bodies. Yes, even you. In my case, it is not my inability to walk or stand that disables me. Rather, I am disabled by the fact that buildings are structured with stairs, narrow hallways, and curbs, making them difficult for me to access on wheels. The public space disables my body, but it could be restructured or reimagined in a way that includes wheelchair and cane users like me. If we had bothered to build ramps, moving around the world in a wheelchair would not be cumbersome; it would be freeing.

In this social model of disability, curing is often unnecessary because the social structures disabling people are healed.

9. Sarah Kim, "The Truth of Disability Employment That No One Talks About," *Forbes*, October 24, 2019, https://www.forbes.com/sites/sarahkim/2019/10/24/sub -minimum-wages-disability.

10. Indigenous scholars and activists Dorothy Lonewolf Miller (Blackfeet) and Jennie R. Joe (Navajo), quoted in Kim Nielsen, *A Disability History of the United States* (Boston: Beacon, 2013), 3.

Constructing buildings and communities with disabled people in mind from the outset produces a culture of belonging that does not discriminate against bodily difference. This model of disability is liberating, because it invites all of us—disabled and nondisabled people alike—to contribute to our neighbors' inclusion and flourishing, regardless of physical differences. Perhaps instead of trying to pray away the cane, prayerful perpetrators should ensure that buildings are accessible to me. Perhaps instead of focusing on my body as the source of sin, prayerful perpetrators should repent for the ways the church perpetuates the sin of excluding disabled people. Perhaps instead of immediately dismissing my body as less valuable, prayerful perpetrators should wonder how my disabled body displays the image of God to our community. Perhaps instead of always attempting to cure, prayerful perpetrators should yearn for holistic healing.

We are tempted to think a magic trick is what we want, but we wouldn't worship a magician.[11] We might pay money to go to a magician's show, or we might follow one on Instagram, but we wouldn't dedicate our lives to worshiping one. Sorry, Penn and Teller. There are no magic pills, quick fixes, or wish-granting genies when it comes to holistic healing. There's Jesus, who wants to be with us: Emmanuel. When we focus too much on curing instead of healing, we reduce the gospel to "good vibes only" merchandise that can be marketed to produce specific, physical results. We're no better than a tacky dietary supplement promising a quick fix. True healing cannot be commodified, no matter what prayerful perpetrators claim. Capitalism likes to attach products to warm and fuzzy feelings to dupe us into believing that we can charge our happiness to a credit card. But healing is not a product that can be bought or sold.

As we learn with Zach in John 9, curing his blindness only worsened his problems. He might be cured, but he is cast out

---

11. I learned this example from a dear friend, teacher, and pastor: Cori Esperanza.

of the community that should bring healing. Curing his blindness doesn't change the social aspects of his disability: exclusion from worship inside the temple, inaccurate perceptions of his sin, and segregation from the broader community. The neighbors still think he was "born entirely in sins" even after Zach is given sight (9:34). True healing would remedy those social aspects of disability instead of abandoning him in social isolation. Healing would remove the stigma of his disability rather than focusing on its physical aspects. Zach goes through a healing process that moves from not knowing who Jesus is, to thinking Jesus is a prophet who can work wonders, to finally realizing Jesus is the Son of Man. His physical cure is the catalyst for this transformation, but it's not the thing that heals him. To focus on his physical journey is to miss what the remainder of the passage teaches us about the social facets of healing.

Whether we like it or not, this passage of Scripture is much more invested in Zach's healing than in his cure. It doesn't offer a magic trick or a solely physical model of disability but reveals disability's deeper social constructs. But of course healing is time-consuming, difficult work, whereas curing is hasty. No wonder prayerful perpetrators would rather demand a quick fix than investigate the way society needs healing when it comes to disability inclusion. As prophet Rachel Held Evans notes, "there is a difference between curing and healing, and the church is called to the slow and difficult work of healing. We are called to enter into one another's pain, anoint the sick, and stick around, no matter the outcome," even when it makes us uncomfortable.[12] Instead of desperately trying to cure all disabilities, the church should do the slow and difficult work of healing the surrounding society by tearing down spaces, practices, and mindsets that are inaccessible to disabled people, even when those spaces are

12. Rachel Held Evans, *Searching for Sunday: Loving, Leaving, and Finding the Church* (Nashville: Nelson, 2015), 208.

inside the church itself. The church should follow Jesus by healing instead of curing.

There's this look that people get when they talk to me about my body. Dewy eyes, cocked head, like they are trying to tenderize a piece of meat. "How are you doooooooooooing?" They trail off, hyperextending the vowel in discomfort. Extended vowels always signal awkwardness. As if adding a few syllables will make you forget I'm disabled. They don't know where to look, what to do with their hands. They think they are the first to recommend a remedy to cure my disability. I've heard everything from "put garlic in your socks" to "drink pickle juice" to "go to a sauna and sweat it out," but my favorite disability remedy from a stranger continues to be "hit your other leg with a hammer." Somehow, I am still disabled.

So many people want to cure me when I've already experienced such rich healing in various forms. My mobility scooter (named "Diana, Princess of the My-Scooter" because I believe that I *am* Wonder Woman), my royal blue cane named Eileen (get what I did there?), and my stumbling gait all proclaim my disability to the world, inviting a scrutinizing gaze that casts my body as public property. "Sleep with soap," they suggest. "Bathe with Epsom salts," she recommends. "Have you tried rubbing herbs on your feet? It helped my cousin . . ." they trail off. People accost me at the grocery store, in Target parking lots, and even in the middle of church, as if everyone has a right to know the intimate details of my medical history whenever they choose. As if my body is a topic of discussion for everyone to share an opinion about. As if I am a problem to be fixed.

This is what it is like to be disabled in an ableist world. We are erased from a society that never wanted us around and continues to use extreme measures to cure us instead of accepting us as we are. I have come to expect this from the medical-industrial complex, because the people caught up in it only know me as medical case file #162742 and not as a human being. Western medicine is set up to treat me as the "before" picture in an elaborate medicinal makeover (working title: *Extreme Makeover: Disabled Edition*). But I refuse to accept this from the body of Christ, whose members are invited to value the diversity of God's creation instead of erasing it. They push cures down my throat without wondering how God is at work through my disability. These moments are always bewildering because they center the experience of the nondisabled person, pitying my disability without knowing anything else about me. I am not waiting for a cure to live an abundant life, and if folks would take the time to get to know me as more than a diagnosis, they would know that.

After each of these "curative" encounters, I find myself wondering what people think would change if I were miraculously cured tomorrow and leaped out of my mobility scooter as the theme song from *Chariots of Fire* blared in the background. Would it make me worship with greater fervor? Would it solidify what I say I believe? Would it give me opportunities that I don't already have to testify to God's love? How would it change my spiritual life—pragmatically? I'm not convinced it would in any meaningful way *other* than highlighting my physical cure in the much larger story about the transformative healing that Jesus brings. I think it would only cause my body to be the center of my praise, instead of prompting me to worship God for who God is.

When strangers desperately covet a cure for my disability, it reveals a deeper discontent about their lack of control over their bodies and lives. After all, Jesus tells us that those who think they can see are the ones who really need healing. Disability is a method of understanding Jesus's ministry and transformative power that is inaccessible to those who are nondisabled. Perhaps this is because disability is a gift, a teacher, and a blessing in Scripture and in life. When we are young and nondisabled, it's easy to buy into the myth that we are in control of our bodies, even though we know deep down that we are not. Subconsciously, we realize that everyone's physical ability is a temporary situation, and that frightens us. I suspect that prayerful perpetrators act out of that fear, projecting onto me their anxiety over a lack of control. Curing offers the illusion of time travel. It promises a ticket to some magical before-time when the fall hadn't "cursed" my body. Cure guarantees fixing—but I don't feel broken.

But cure also offers *them* a ticket to travel away from this moment where they are confronted by lingering questions about theodicy and God's will. Or worse. What if *they* become disabled? By either age or accident, most people will experience some form of disability in their lives. Those of us who already live in its company know how to welcome it, how to learn from it, how to witness God at work in it. We, the disabled, bear prophetic witness about what is true about the fragile human condition. If only the church would listen to us.

Throughout Scripture, we encounter disabled people at the forefront of the work that God chooses to do with humanity. Isaac became blind. Jacob walks with a limp. Leah has "weak eyes" (Gen. 29:17 NIV). Moses has a speech disorder. Elijah feels depressed and suicidal. Timothy has stomach issues and "frequent ailments" (1 Tim. 5:23). Paul has the thorn in the flesh (2 Cor. 12:7). And who can forget Mephibosheth's two lame feet? The Good Shepherd brings abundant life, with and without our bodies being "able" or cured. God's healing is not contingent on our physical state. And according to John 9, it is Zach's blindness that displays God to the community, not his miraculous sight. Perhaps if we started to consider disability as a way to reveal the living God, prayerful perpetrators wouldn't accost me at church with their magician theology.

We need to disentangle ourselves from any system that claims there is a hierarchy of bodies and minds. We already have a context for this in the rest of creation. We expect there to be variety when it comes to trees, flowers, and animals, just not humans. There are sixty thousand types of trees, three thousand varieties of tulips, and four hundred kinds of sharks. No one claims fringed tulips are better or worse than cup-shaped tulips. They are both beautiful in their distinctiveness.

We need to start thinking about bodies in the same way we think about tulips. No body is better or worse than another body because it is fringed or cupped. Variety isn't just the spice of life; it sustains life. Variation allows organisms to survive. Instead of eradicating difference, we should celebrate it.

Imagine if you never compared your body to others'. Wouldn't that be liberating? To embrace your body for what it can do and how unique it is rather than admonish it for not being tall enough, thin enough, strong enough, fast enough, smart enough (or whatever your "enough" is). Imagine how healing it would be if you celebrated yourself as a fringed tulip and stopped trying to become a cup-shaped tulip, without belittling either one.

My disabled body is beautiful in its distinctiveness. My body might be more crooked than yours, but it has earned its spiky edges. My leg might be blue from lack of circulation, but it sparkles like sapphires. My nerves are on fire, but it is fire that releases the sequoia cones that germinate the forest. My spasms are as sharp as ice, but ice is what regulates the ocean's tide. My disabled body is made of the same stuff as stars.

It is time for us to experience the world as a sea of three thousand different tulips and embrace the radiance and beauty of all tulips shining beneath the same sun.

REFLECTION AND RESPONSE

▶ Reflect. What is your initial response to disabled people? Do you try to cure us, pity us, or condescend to us? Are you

open to the ways disabled people might teach you? Reflect
on how your own relationship to disability might make you
defensive as you absorb the stories and lessons of this book.
Discuss your reflections with a friend, small group, or someone in your community to develop mutual accountability.

▶ Take the Harvard Implicit Association Test for disability:
https://implicit.harvard.edu/implicit/selectatest.html. It
takes about eight to ten minutes to complete.

Reflect on your result or share it with trusted people in
your community. We learn about our implicit bias not to
blame or shame ourselves but to name the bias that we might
have absorbed from the culture in which we are immersed.
Instead of using the test as a destination, use it as a point of
departure from which to grow and learn, making sure that
you don't let any bias ossify.

▶ Do an inventory of your church or group's gathering space
and etiquette toward disabled people. Is it accessible, including bathrooms, parking, and preaching spaces? Does the liturgy allow for different physical and sensory needs (including the needs of those who are blind or low vision, d/Deaf,
wheelchair users, and autistic)? Is the song choice, exegesis,
and theology inclusive to disabled people? Does your church
encourage and mentor disabled people to lead? If your inventory reveals the need for growth, commit to changing these
aspects to allow your church to embody the 2 Corinthians
church where all members of the body are valued.

TOP TEN
Recommended Remedies

Strangers recommend these "treatments" for my disability.

10. Sleep with a bar of soap.

9. Put garlic in your socks.

8. Get more sun. Avoid the sun. Become a vampire and never see the sun again.

7. Put a heat lamp on your leg. Put ice packs on your leg.

6. Bathe with Epsom salts. This will draw out the disability.

5. Take vitamin C, magnesium, iron, or sometimes all three at once, just for fun.

4. Drink bone broth or pickle juice. (But not together. *Never* together.)

3. Try to relax.

2. Try jogging. After a while, your legs will remember how to walk.

1. Hit your other leg with a hammer to take your mind off the pain.

Disability Discrimination

My high school campus was huge. The red and white concrete stucco facades spanned enough land to enclose four Rose Bowls. Our campus was twice the size of Ellis Island. Between classes, three thousand bodies traversed the tree-lined quad, like a stampede of wildebeests across the Maasai Mara. To offset navigating this commotion in a manual wheelchair, I asked my teachers if I could arrive three minutes late to class.

"No," my teacher chided in front of the entire class. "We don't want you goofing off and taking advantage of arriving late. That would be unfair to the other students." Several tardy tickets and trips to the principal's office later, my parents asked the school administration for this minor disability accommodation, without success.

A seat by the door was also denied. "We can't give *you* preferential treatment just because you're in a wheelchair," we were educated.

When I had to miss class every Thursday for medical procedures, my calculus teacher refused to let me make up the quizzes. "You need to take class more seriously," she said. I'm not sure how "serious" I could take it. I'd much rather be learning math (yes, even *math*) than getting injections in my spine.

"You can't have accommodations in advanced classes," my chemistry teacher scolded. One teacher suggested I move to a remedial class for "special" students because disabled students "can't keep up in advanced classes." Others simply refused to comply with federally mandated accommodations.

That's what led my parents, teachers, and principal to pile into a crowded, beige office with no natural light or ventilation one frosty morning. The tension in the room was thick. No one wanted to be there, least of all me. The scent of stale Starbucks lingered in the air from my teacher's breakfast latte as he rolled his eyes, more than once, at the meeting cutting into his morning prep. Another of my teachers burst through the door, tardy, broadcasting through narrowed eyes that it was demanding too much for him to make a 7 a.m. conference because he was not paid for this.

The purpose of the meeting was to create an educational plan best suited to the disabled student. Parents, educators, and school psychiatrists might have differed about the logistics, but the goal was to work together and implement a strategy to ensure that the disabled student would receive education comparable to that of nondisabled students. At least, that was the goal on paper. My teachers had no interest in working with me or my parents, and they didn't bother cloaking their sour attitude in saccharine smiles or empty platitudes. "We've never dealt with this before" is something we heard on repeat. As if novelty is an excuse to deny someone's civil rights.

My teachers had no experience dealing with IEPs (individualized education programs), 504s, and all other disability-related acronyms. They made no effort to educate themselves. Ironic, right? They yearned for me to drop advanced classes and become someone else's problem. I know because they told me. Repeatedly. In front of other students. What's worse, they blamed me—with punitive tardy marks, trips to the principal's office, and spiteful comments—for daring to hold them accountable to federal law.[1]

My teachers seemed to think of accommodations as an add-on, like the additional charge for guacamole at Chipotle. But civil rights are not guacamole. Late arrival, make-up tests, and accessible seating are all standard disability accommodations central to a student's ability to learn. These are not optional, nor should they be denied on the basis of cost, convenience, or ignorance.

I should have been every teacher's dream. There was no assignment or reading I didn't do. No paper I didn't revise three times. No extra credit opportunity I didn't take. When I found out my blood type was A positive, I was thrilled because "A+ runs in my veins," I announced to my brother. I *cherished* school. It was a large part of who I believed I was. So being on the receiving end of teachers' ire was terrifying for adolescent me.

"Forgive them, for they know not what they do," Jesus prayed. But my teachers *did* know what they were doing. They were informed that they were breaking the law in our awkward, pre-class conferences. They did it anyway.

"I'll prove them wrong," I steadied myself, revenge music blaring in the background. Every snide remark about disability only added fuel to the fire of my determination. I believed I could change my educators' minds because I had right on my side. I thought that if I was smart enough, hardworking enough, and achieved enough, I could make them value disabled people. I thought that I could perfectionist my way out of disability discrimination.

I was caught somewhere between being a burden and a supercrip, trying to prove them wrong: that disability does not

1. For more on disability rights laws for students in public schools, check out the fact sheet from the ADA National Network, "Disability Rights Laws in Public Primary and Secondary Education: How Do They Relate?," 2018, https://adata.org/factsheet /disability-rights-laws-public-primary-and-secondary-education-how-do-they-relate.

mean I am worthless or incapable of contributing (burden), but if I topple over into the realm of contributing so much that people forget about my disability altogether, they may believe I "overcame" my disability and deny accommodations (supercrip). "Crip" is a disability community word that reclaims the slur "cripple" in hopes of transforming the way the world interprets our bodies. Sometimes being cast as a supercrip means people refuse to acknowledge the accommodations I need to survive (let alone thrive). I was trapped on the hamster wheel of performing my worth, my body an "in spite of" instead of a contributing ally in my life.

Fast-forward to an academic rally at the end of the school year. "Celebrate good times" muffled the melody of shoes squeaking across the basketball court. Teachers and students cheered as awards were given to those with the highest grade point averages in the school. Top Ten, we called this group: the most prestigious academic club on campus, where all of us nerds got to feel like superstars for a day. Posters unfurled from the ceiling, revealing who made the cut. There was my name, among the top ten GPAs in the entire school. My misty eyes stared down my name as balloons and confetti snowballed. The confetti would be stuck in my wheels for weeks to come. Being in Top Ten suddenly meant nothing.

All those late nights solving differential equations in between hallucinogenic drugs and experimental nerve stimulation. All those digestive system flash cards rehearsed in the car on the way to the neurologist. All those internal flames I fanned to prove my adversarial teachers wrong for not providing accommodations—they were completely extinguished. I remained in the Top Ten, but it did nothing to shift my teachers' already ossified notions about disability. The only thing that changed was the amount of sleep I got.

I burned myself out. When I tell you I was burned out, I mean that I was getting six hours of sleep per week, my medications burned a hole in my esophagus, and I went periodically blind from the invasive and experimental medical procedures. "Burned out" doesn't begin to communicate the levels of destruction done to my body that year in the name of health care and education.

I wish I could go back and tell my younger self that I didn't need to prove my educators wrong. That no number of academic awards or posters with my name on them or any inner-vengeance incinerator (ven-cinerator?) was going to change my teachers' minds. I wish I could make her understand that their bias wasn't about me in any way, that it was forged out of preconceived notions that disability is inferior. I wish I could tell her that she is enough.

But I was sixteen, and I wouldn't have listened. That's the thing about being a type A know-it-all. We rarely heed others who might know better. We must learn the lesson by braving the blaze ourselves. The fire did refine me, but not without a few scalding burns. My teachers taught me a lot that year, but not about calculus or chemistry. What I learned won't be found in any textbook, and I probably couldn't have learned it without burning myself out in the name of proving them wrong. The fire taught me that no amount of hard work or determination can "overcome" my disability and that there are people who will perpetuate ableism despite the suffering it causes me. That working twice as hard to prove them wrong only burned me out.

What my teachers did was illegal and morally wrong. They dismissed my disability accommodations and ignored my civil rights. Why? Because they could. But they were not the true antagonist in my story. My antagonist was the core spiritual lie that I needed to prove my worth through hard work, intelligence, or belonging to a prestigious academic club. That my 4.6 GPA was my identity. That my ability to "overcome" made me valuable. My teachers had believed this lie, and for a while I did too. I thought I *was* my GPA and nerdy Top Ten accolades.

Or, at the very least, I thought that they were what endowed me with worth. That somehow I could outsmart the fact that I was—and still am—disabled.

My teachers ignored explicit federal mandates about how to accommodate my disability, which makes their ableist behavior easy to identify, because it directly violated laws intended to protect disabled students. But most ableism lurks beneath the surface. It lingers in conversations where the assumption is that being disabled is tragic, burdensome, and worthless. It coats itself in pity and euphemism to make itself seem less toxic. It seeps into our thinking without us even realizing.

It is convenient to think that ableism is something that happens "out there," in a distant land full of cartoon villains who despise disabled people and openly plot our demise. (Insert evil laugh here.) But ableism is much broader than that. Ableism is "a system that places value on people's bodies and minds based on societally constructed ideas of normalcy, intelligence, excellence, and productivity."[2] It claims that some bodies are better than others. It values people only for what they produce. It suggests our résumés and our GPAs are more important than our humanity. It withholds belonging until we prove we are worthy of it.

Ableism is not a character trait, an identity, or an illness. It is a system that starts with a philosophy. The Western philosophy of Aristotle, to be precise. Aristotle claimed that disabled people lacked reason and therefore were subhuman. His hierarchy of humanity has been used as the basis for racist, sexist, and ableist philosophies that are still pervasive today.[3]

---

2. A working definition by Talila A. Lewis, "Ableism 2020: An Updated Definition," January 25, 2020, https://www.talilalewis.com/blog/ableism-2020-an-updated-definition.

3. Thank you to Lisa Sharon Harper for encouraging me to include this, and thanks to her, Shannon Dingle, and Lisa Anderson for discussing this with me on "Disability and Its Intersections," 2020, *Freedom Road*, podcast, https://freedomroad.us/2020/06/2231.

Actions, words, and ideas can be ableist. In my experience, ableist ideas are not always premeditated or purposeful. They are part of the script we've been handed by a society not built for every body-mind.[4] Thanks, Aristotle. Pervasive and invisible, ableism is so deeply woven into the fabric of our ideas about what is "normal" and "good" that we barely even notice it is there. Once you start to notice ableism, you will witness it everywhere. I do mean *every*where. It is difficult *not* to maintain ableist practices because they are so ingrained into our individualistic, "pull-yourself-up-by-your-bootstraps" society. Ableism is all around.

But, unlike an illness, ableism can be selected or rejected. We might not have realized it was there to begin with, but once we do recognize it, we can choose to stop upholding its harmful ideas and practices. We can choose to honor the least of these by changing our language and behaviors. We can choose to live in a way that reflects what we believe: everybody is an image-bearer regardless of ability or accolades.

The most harmful ableism I have experienced has been inside the church. I can almost understand it from my teachers and employers. People have been taught to value product over personhood, profit over people, and cash as king above all else. Disabled people do not produce anything the capitalist market deems valuable, and therefore we are cast aside as drains on the system. It's eugenicist, but that's capitalism. Eugenics tells us we can "improve" humanity by getting rid of any traits we find undesirable, an idea that has been used to justify forced sterilization, medical experimentation, and murder, particularly of disabled people, Jewish people, poor people, and people of

4. "Body-mind" is a term used in the disability community as a way to counteract mind/body dualism.

color. Our modern notions of strength and morality are rooted in a system that values some bodies over others.

But churches are meant to usher in new creation where all people have dignity and value simply because we are image-bearers of the Alpha and the Omega. Churches peddle ableist ideas in sneaky ways. Many churches claim to be "pro-life," but they mirror ableist messaging that productivity and health are the drivers of dignity and worth. Many churches weaponize prayer, reducing God to a slimy vending machine churning out magical miracles upon request. One bendy body, coming right up! Just name it and claim it. "Jesus didn't die for you to be in a wheelchair," I've been told more times than I can count.

Many churches limit our imaginations for how abundant life *should* function, as if prosperity and happiness are confined to a party in a music video. They create ministries *to* disabled people, casting us as a group of second-class citizens who must be segregated from the general congregation, never considering that disabled people have something to teach the broader community about living an embodied faith, never realizing that we are not objects of pity and charity but image-bearers with our own gifts to share with the beloved community. Many churches blame eschatology for dehumanizing "worship" songs that claim to praise the living God while mocking the beautiful diversity of God's creation. They avoid the discomfort of a messy lived experience by constantly promising a completeness yet to come. "You'll be whole one day" or "you'll be running in heaven," they promise through pursed lips, as though I am not already a new creation with the mind of Christ. As if the Holy Spirit doesn't already dwell in my disabled body.

It is no wonder that many of our churches have absorbed the core spiritual lie known as ableism, when the landmark legislation that provided civil rights for disabled people in the United States is something that some Christian communities fought against. Alongside chanting "come just as you are" and blasting

"WWJD" on every bracelet, mug, and T-shirt, many Christian spaces petitioned to exclude disabled people. When the Americans with Disabilities Act (ADA) was signed into law in 1990, it excluded religious communities after some Christian leaders lobbied for restrictions.

Now, the ADA is not all it's cracked up to be. I have visited bookstores where there is no disability parking, supermarkets where my mobility scooter can't fit through the aisles, and restaurants without accessible bathrooms. Even the law allows for exceptions based on the historical significance of a building, as if architecture is more important than inclusion. What's even more aggravating is that the ADA isn't enforceable. Not in any real sense, anyway. There is no governing body that certifies ADA compliance before businesses open, nor one that shuts down businesses that refuse to follow the law.

The ADA is enforced only via lawsuits. Imagine if health code violations operated in the same way. You'd suffer through a nasty bout of salmonella before anyone bothered to check if the restaurant cooked your chicken fingers. Then you'd wait for months to sue the restaurant, longing to win your case, before anything was done about it. All the while, other folks would endure the same preventable food poisoning without any consequences for the restaurant. This wouldn't really inspire you to order the chicken—not knowing if it comes with a side of salmonella. So no, the ADA doesn't solve everything.

But for all its flaws and lack of enforcement, the ADA was a huge win for the disability community. Outside the church, that is. The law that finally granted accessible bathrooms, curb cuts, and ramps in public spaces was vehemently condemned by some Christian churches and schools as "imposing burdensome costs . . . [and] needless injury to religious exercise."[5]

5. William B. Ball, letter to William L. Roper, July 13, 1989, available at http:// dolearchivecollections.ku.edu/collections/ada/files/s-leg_753_001_all.pdf (p. 109).

The message was clear: we are simply not worth the cost. Money was more important than disabled people. Camel, meet eye of needle. Evidently, our very presence diminished the ability of others to worship. Representing the Association of Christian Schools International, attorney William B. Ball argued that "nothing can be clearer than that the free exercise of religion will be seriously impaired by imposing the ADA on religious bodies."[6] Writing on behalf of the National Association of Evangelicals, Robert P. Dugan Jr. claimed the ADA defied religious liberty, even going as far as to call it "a particular odious affront" that would "violate our faith commitments."[7] Even today, churches and religious schools are not legally required to follow the ADA. Every disabled parking space at a church, every accessible bathroom at a private school, every ramp to the sanctuary has been included out of benevolence, not because of the core belief that disabled people are equal and should be endowed with the same basic civil rights as everyone else. Ableism is not a system bug but a calculated feature in many churches in the United States. The erasure of disability in church spaces was deliberately manufactured because disabled people were (and still are) considered too pricey and profane to include. Knowing that houses of worship argued that including my body is offensive to their religious liberty will always sting. Knowing that this is still the law today cuts deeper. (Pricey and Profane sounds like a cool band name, though.)

When churches withhold full humanity from disabled people, they perpetuate the notion that disability is a defect in the perfect race of humans. Unwittingly or not, they participate in a discourse of eugenics, suggesting that some bodies contain more worth than others. From the Holocaust to the halls of Congress, disabled people have been expunged without

6. Ball to Roper, July 13, 1989.
7. Robert P. Dugan Jr., letter to Senator Tom Harkin, July 14, 1989, http://dole archivecollections.ku.edu/collections/ada/files/s-leg_753_001_all.pdf (p. 114).

most people so much as noticing. Behind a scratched partition in a dank room at Auschwitz lies a red left leg with canary-colored knee joints and a brass shoe. A right leg with frayed crimson fabric still clinging to the shin. A right forearm with a flaxen hand. Canes. Crutches. Braces. Wheelchairs. These artifacts are all that remain of lives deemed worthy of sacrifice for the "superior" race—mangled, discarded, and torn off of bodies to create a sea of artificial limbs behind a glass case. Lives reduced to piles of rejected rubble. Nazis used the term "useless eaters" to refer to the 275,000 disabled people they massacred.[8]

In our modern discourse, we've replaced "useless eater" with dog-whistles like "quality of life," "special needs," and "mercy killing," perverting the concept of mercy to justify murder. "Never again," we swear, blissfully unaware that more than 110,000 people in the US died awaiting their disability payments in the past decade alone, and every week in North America a disabled child is murdered by parents, relatives, or caregivers simply for being disabled.[9] Burdens, they call us. As the bodies pile up, disabled people are withered to a catalog of things that can be resold in a market that rejected us. There is no space for us to thrive in a society that deems us burdens. We are chewed up and spit out without anyone even noticing that we are belched. The outcome of ableism is eugenics. The body of Christ must decide whether it truly values life enough to change its exclusionary ways and embrace disabled people like me.

8. United States Holocaust Memorial Museum, "People with Disabilities," accessed September 8, 2021, https://www.ushmm.org/collections/bibliography/people-with-disabilities.

9. Aimee Picchi, "Almost 110,000 Americans Died While Waiting for a Social Security Disability Hearing," CBS News, August 14, 2020, https://www.cbsnews.com/news/disability-benefits-gao-report-death-bankruptcies-waiting-hearings. For statistics on violence against disabled people, including filicide, check out David Perry, "The Ruderman White Paper on Media Coverage of the Murder of People with Disabilities by Their Caregivers," Ruderman Family Foundation, March 2017, https://rudermanfoundation.org/wp-content/uploads/2017/08/Murders-by-Caregivers-WP_final_final.pdf.

Christian leaders fighting against the ADA is recent history, and yet very few people seem to know about it. That's how ableism works. It erases us from the pages of history to keep folks ignorant about the way disabled people are treated. Ableism lurks in the shadows, and most folks assume everything is fine since they don't know about it. Whenever I share any of this history with people, they are shocked. Alarmed. Outraged! It seems outside the realm of possibility, as if I have just suggested that dogs perform brain surgery. You wouldn't trust a spaniel with a scalpel!

The underlying assumption is that ableism doesn't exist. Sure, there are Scrooges out there, but most folks would never *intentionally* hurt disabled people, they promise me. The accepted response is disbelief. It's like trying to explain gravity to a bubble. Any time I talk about ableism, someone is quick to point out that that's just the way things are, as though "the way things are" is naturally occurring, like the ocean's tide. Complacency is the hardest hurdle to clear. Many people reassure me that systems are just like that; no one intends any harm. Setting aside the lack of imagination about more inclusive ways to structure our world, I am not convinced this is true.

The way that ableism works so brilliantly is to make itself invisible. It is the air we breathe, the water we swim in, the culture we all consume. It becomes automatic and uninterrogated, so we don't even realize we are worshiping idols of success and self-sufficiency rather than the living God. Ableist ideas about some bodies bearing more of God's image than others linger like an app in the background; we don't even notice that we are giving energy to sustaining their existence. This deceives us into thinking ableism is natural and therefore unavoidable.

Perhaps we are content with deceiving ourselves because if we admitted the reality of ableism, then we'd have to do something about it. It is easier to dismiss, doubt, and deny. All the while, disabled people are exterminated and erased. As I write this in

2021, disabled people do not have minimum wage, voting access, or marriage equality in the United States.[10] We are trotted out for photo ops and feel-good vignettes every election cycle, and then quickly hidden to ensure no one becomes too "uncomfortable" with our wayward bodies. Friends don't usually say this part out loud, but most people think it if they're honest. Just ask the poll from chapter 1. Our very existence makes people uncomfortable. Between inspirational videos, disabled people are relegated to the shadows, where most people simply forget about us. We are erased from the pages of history, with no one left to tell our story.

I carry all of this with me as I travel about the world: too much emotional baggage to fit in an overhead compartment. Our churches, whether they have intended to or not, have consumed ableist ideology and discriminated against disabled people. If our churches really want to be salt and light, they should cultivate different habits not infused by this limited notion of disability. We have worshiped at the altar of nondisabled bodies for far too long. It is time to dismantle these idols, repent of discrimination, and allow disability to teach us. To those of us feeling convicted (or defensive), think of this not as a destination, but a departure. Grace to you, friend. If you didn't know this history, don't waste time trying to explain or excuse. Instead of responding with self-protection, choose to learn and grow alongside us. Now is the time to depart from upholding ableist practices and follow the way of Jesus, who centered the least of these.

10. US Department of Labor, "Fact Sheet #39: The Employment of Workers with Disabilities at Subminimum Wages," July 2008, https://www.dol.gov/agencies/whd/fact-sheets/39-14c-subminimum-wage.

Jesus gives us a model for how we should treat disabled people. It is not about being nice or politically correct. This is how Jesus will know us. When explaining how the "sheep" will be separated from the "goats," Jesus tells us, "Truly I tell you, just as you did it to one of the least of these who are members of my family, you did it to me" (Matt. 25:40). Sometimes we want to overspiritualize this verse. We imagine how mystical Jesus is. Or we use the phrase as a litmus test for how holy we are.

But really, when we quote this verse, we should be thinking about the incarnation. Jesus knows what it's like to be a poor, marginalized refugee who suffered at the hands of a powerful empire. Telling us that we harm Jesus when we harm outcasts isn't theoretical. It's incarnational. Jesus commands us to care for the "least of these," offering a model of corporate solidarity with humanity. This command reveals how collective humanity has supported Jesus when we care for the outcast, the poor, the lame, the orphan, or the sojourner. The righteous aren't even aware that they are feeding, clothing, and visiting Jesus. They even question *when* they did this, because they were doing that for humanity. They are just as surprised as we are. The righteous don't need to be aware because Jesus is with every downtrodden outcast that we encounter.

This is how Jesus describes the difference between those who will be given eternal life and those who will receive eternal punishment. Jesus doesn't lead everyone in the sinner's prayer or hand out a tract with the four spiritual laws. Jesus invites us to care for the least of these. When I read this passage, I picture Jesus telling the church who fought against the ADA: "Depart from me, for I was in a wheelchair and you gave me no ramp; I was d/Deaf, and you gave me no interpreter; I was blind, and you gave me no visual descriptions. I needed an accessible bathroom, and you did not install one because it was too expensive. I asked you not to insult me by saying 'lame' and you laughed at me. I wanted to be included, and you said it would violate your faith commitments. I was disabled, and you did not accommodate me" (cf. Matt. 25:41–43). How we treat disabled people is how we treat Jesus. Too bad Jesus makes two-thirds of us uncomfortable.

In many modern churches, you can attend a Sunday service without ever interacting with a disabled person. The nondisabled person cannot say to a disabled person, "I have no need of you" (1 Cor. 12:21). How preposterous would that be? We cannot treat parts of the body of Christ as disposable. All too often, churches have functioned in this way, removing disabled people from their services through whispers and side-glances. Disruptive, they call us. Pretending that befriending disabled people is a unique calling only bestowed on the most patient among us. Creating services and socials that segregate disabled people instead of asking the rest of the body of Christ to learn from us. Foisting us off on someone else, so we are not too unruly in the main service. Separate yet equal is never equal. This segregation is an extension of churches fighting against the ADA.

If your service is more focused on silencing disruption than it is on welcoming the least of these, then you are not welcoming Jesus. It may sound harsh, and it might even hurt a few feelings, but no sermon or liturgy or song is more important than disabled people belonging. A person's feelings of discomfort should never be in competition with someone else's belonging. Church could be a sacred space where "everyone is safe, but no one is comfortable."[11] Get used to the holy disruption. Get used to having your expectations shattered. Get used to treating us as humans instead of projects. Only then might you catch a whisper of the groans too deep to utter. Only then might you encounter the living God among the least of these.

11. Rachel Held Evans, *Searching for Sunday: Loving, Leaving, and Finding the Church* (Nashville: Nelson, 2015), 73.

It is time for us to repair what ableism has broken. Ableism hurts everyone. Yes, even you. Ranking and categorizing bodies and minds is harmful to us all. Sure, it hurts those of us who are disabled first, but eventually, it will come for you too. Are you "able-bodied"? Or are you just temporarily nondisabled? If you live long enough, your body will likely experience disability in one way or another. Are you any less worthy of dignity and respect in those moments when your body-mind functions differently than it once did? Do you bear less of God's image? The truth is that everyone's ability is a temporary condition. The more you learn to live in the company of disability, the more you can embrace it when it finally comes for you. That's not a threat, but a promise. Perhaps that's the real fear loitering beneath the discomfort with disabled people: the realization that you, too, will likely join us one day. We are the mirror you don't want to see. We embody the future that you are afraid to imagine. Maybe you should learn from us instead of casting us aside.

Disabled people are the canaries in the coal mine, we often say in crip spaces. Miners used canaries to detect carbon monoxide and other invisible gases. If the canaries continued to sing, the miners were safe. Once the canaries stopped singing, the miners were warned: Get out, now! Silence is the signal.

Our vibrant yellow and green feathers highlight the way we jut out in a gray world not made for us. But we shouldn't have to die to make our reality known. We are singing an urgent song of truth to the church about its ableist structures that will eventually harm all of us. Will you listen?

REFLECTION AND RESPONSE

▶ Lead your church, friends, or community in repentance, acknowledging the harm done by the church in fighting against the ADA. This is not to shame people but to generate awareness and invite nondisabled people into considering the impact of this segregation. Confession and repentance are regular practices of spiritual formation. Acknowledging the harm and committing to reducing that harm helps create solidarity between disabled and nondisabled people.

▶ For nondisabled people: Join a Disability Day of Mourning to participate in corporate lament with the disability community. For a list of resources and events, check out the Disability Day of Mourning website, https://disability -memorial.org.

▶ For fellow disabled people: Remember a time when someone said or did something ableist toward you. Re-create the narrative with words, pictures, or meditations in a way that reimagines the event without ableism. This is not to minimize the harm or accept the ableism, but to try to edit the event in your mind to imagine how God might reassure you of your own belovedness in that moment. How might God remind you of how beloved you are? What would you want to be called instead of the ableist word? How would you want to be treated? Sit in the feeling of the edited moment, emphasizing your own worth and value to the God who sees.

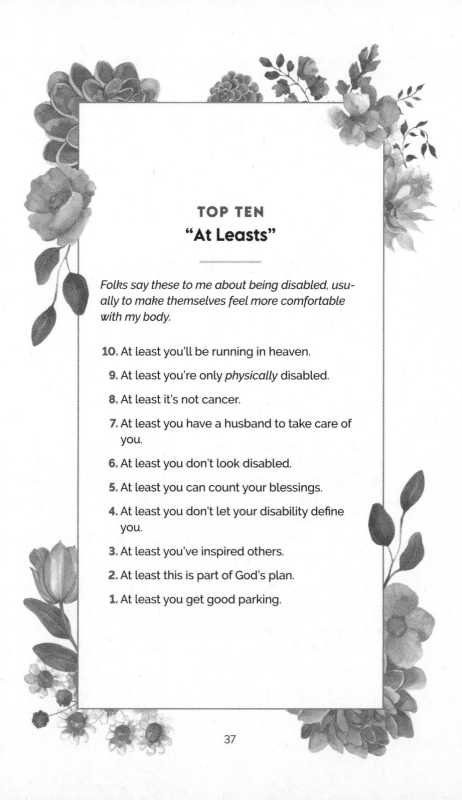

TOP TEN
"At Leasts"

Folks say these to me about being disabled, usually to make themselves feel more comfortable with my body.

10. At least you'll be running in heaven.

9. At least you're only *physically* disabled.

8. At least it's not cancer.

7. At least you have a husband to take care of you.

6. At least you don't look disabled.

5. At least you can count your blessings.

4. At least you don't let your disability define you.

3. At least you've inspired others.

2. At least this is part of God's plan.

1. At least you get good parking.

Disability Doubters

I'm determined to make my trip to the DMV as swift as possible. How long can it take to renew my disabled plates? Unfortunately, the exasperated employee renewing disabled license plates didn't get the memo. I shuffle through my forms, the navy plastic chair sticking to the back of my legs as I wait to be summoned. Vehicle registration—check. Doctor's note—check. Form 195 verifying that I have "impaired mobility in one or more extremities" and a "diagnosed disease that substantially interferes with mobility"—check. A licensed medical provider's certification of disability—check. Fear I will encounter another disability doubter—check.

"G7 to window 24," the loudspeaker commands. I hobble over to the cubicle on the other side of the room like a race walker at the Olympics. "Why do *you* need a disabled plate?" she quizzes, making heads turn. She asks so many questions that it puts toddlers to shame: "Where is form 195?" "Where is your certification of disability?" "Where is your doctor's note?" Ten minutes later, I have produced all the forms verifying I am disabled, and not just using a cane for kicks. There is nothing left for her to do but humiliate me. "If you were *really* disabled, you wouldn't be able to drive," she scolds.

She won't renew my disabled plates until I pass her arbitrary test of removing my current disabled license plates. "If you *tried* hard enough," she says, "you'd be able to." Blink, blink, blink, blink, I count in my head, unsure how to respond, trying to blink away my irritation. It's like we're reenacting the sloth scene from *Zootopia*, except there isn't a punch line rewarding us at the end of the awkward suspension.

A slender stranger, wearing a tank top that reveals more tattoos than skin, approaches what is now becoming a scene. "Can *I* change your plates for you?" he offers, compassion beaming from his chestnut eyes. My new friend is fresh out of prison. As he unscrews my plates, he spills that he knows what it's like to be dismissed by the system and wants to support a fellow outcast.

And it's there, in a DMV parking lot on top of crumbling cement, that I am met with more accommodations than I have found in most churches. Jesus showed up in the form of an eavesdropping ex-felon that day. Jesus is always showing up for me like that, whenever disability doubters linger nearby. I just wish Jesus would hang out at church more often. Maybe then my disabled body could belong.

There's this episode of *Law & Order: Special Victims Unit* where Benson and Stabler's investigation leads them to interview the prime suspect, Linus McKellen, and his wife, Tessa, who uses a wheelchair.[1] In the dramatic final minutes of the episode, Benson and Stabler discover that Linus hasn't accompanied Tessa to the neurologist for many years out of guilt

1. *Law & Order: Special Victims Unit*, season 7, episode 15, "Manipulated," aired February 7, 2006.

over driving the night of the accident that caused her paralysis and—plot twist—she might not need to use a wheelchair any longer. Could it be true? There's only one way to find out. Linus shoves his wife, wheelchair and all, into the pool. Gasp. Benson and Stabler stare down at the water. Abruptly, Tessa kicks. It turns out she's been faking all along. Evidently her husband could be cajoled into staying with her as a "nurse-maid" only if she pretended to rely on a wheelchair to get around. Sigh.

It's not just *Law & Order: Special Victims Unit*. *The Brady Bunch*, *Castle*, *Doctor Who*, *Frasier*, *Game of Thrones*, *Glee*, *Happy Endings*, *House*, *How I Met Your Mother*, *Jane the Virgin*, *Modern Family*, *Monk*, *Murder, She Wrote*, *New Girl*, *The Office*, *Pushing Daisies*, *Seinfeld*, *A Series of Unfortunate Events*, *Sherlock*, *Smallville*, *Sons of Anarchy*, *30 Rock*, *The Wire*, and *The X-Files* have all used the faking disability trope as well. And those are just some of the TV shows guilty of using this trope! Characters pretend to be disabled to scam the system in some way, gaining a settlement, a spouse, or sympathy from the charade.

This plot twist might seem harmless in a serial crime drama, but the suspicion that someone is faking disability for emotional or financial gain spills over into the real world. It perpetuates skepticism of all disabled people, casting us as "fakers, takers, and moneymakers."[2] People are so convinced that behind every cane is a con that they interrogate us without cause.

"Did you get separated from your party?" A sturdy, bald, menacing man asks me. His Hawaiian print and straggly flip-flops reveal he's not a Disney employee. He's simply a beefy bystander, intruding because I don't meet his random qualifications for disabled.

---

2. Rebecca Cockley, quoted in Andrew Pulrang, "We Need to Stop Patrolling the Borders of Disability," *Forbes*, June 30, 2020, https://www.forbes.com/sites/andrewpulrang/2020/06/30/we-need-to-stop-patrolling-the-borders-of-disability.

To navigate Disneyland's cobblestoned terrain and windy stairs, I register for a guest assistance pass, a ticket to the stair-free route for the rides. Step-free access requires entering rides like Indiana Jones Adventure through the exit, where hordes of explorers inform me "you're going the wrong *way*" as I snake my way to a series of concealed elevators. "Where does she think *she's* going?" they grumble in my direction.

I ignore them, and I want to avoid this Hawaiian-clad man, but I don't feel safe enough to dismiss him outright. "Nope," is what I summon in response to his grilling, before I turn away to hamper future dialogue. He shifts his weight, puffing up his chest to enhance his dominance. "Well, I didn't see a wheelchair. This entrance is for disabled people only." His coffee breath bathes the cramped space between us.

This man—this defender of disabled purity—does not know anything about my disability; all he perceives is an opportunity to shame me publicly. He is one of a dozen interrogators I endure that day. Evidently the Happiest Place on Earth doesn't include disabled people. Turns out the glittery fireworks, Mickey-shaped funnel cakes, and overly cheerful renditions of "It's a Small World (After All)" blasting from the speakers can't shift the guests' doubts about disability.

Other times, disability doubters are more official. They use gratuitous form-filling to do their insidious interrogations for them. I had just moved into an apartment complex that advertised itself as "wheelchair accessible" and promised disabled parking. When I inquired further, the landlords become cagey. "We *want* to help," one landlord backtracked, "but we don't want to *inconvenience* the other residents by giving you preferential treatment. You understand."

I understand refusing disability accommodations perfectly. So did the Department of Housing and Urban Development (HUD) when I called to file a complaint under the Fair Housing Act. Almost as soon as I had hung up the phone, the paperwork flooded in. One form requested medical professionals to verify that I am, in fact, disabled, and not just using a mobility scooter out of "laziness." Their word. Another admonished that my disability cannot "include sexual behavior disorders, compulsive gambling, kleptomania, pyromania, or psychoactive substance use disorders." It doesn't, but why is any of that my landlord's business? I'm not sure how bookmaking relates to requiring accessible parking. Accommodations should not be a gamble. A third form asked me to specify why this accommodation was "reasonable" and how it would help me "live here as successfully as the other residents." The list goes on: paperwork as long as a CVS receipt.

At the time I was using a wheelchair full time, had disabled plates on my car (thanks to my eavesdropping ex-felon friend), and held a disabled placard, all of which had to be medically certified. I could not stand for more than two minutes at a time, even with Eileen, my cane. My left leg was withered, blue, and spasmic. All of this is to say that my disability was visible and legible to anyone who so much as glanced my way. There was no reason that my disability needed further endorsement—the paperwork was only for intimidation purposes. The apartment complex was swimming in documentation proving I was disabled, but that didn't stop the landlords from asking for forms on forms. Who was going to stop them? Excessive paperwork was a means to justify administrative ableism.

After weeks of back-and-forth and after I filed a complaint with HUD and the Department of Justice to demonstrate that parking spaces are reasonable accommodations under the Fair Housing Act, the apartment complex finally acquiesced. Sort of. The landlords did not reassign someone else's parking space or even provide a space dedicated to disability parking; they simply provided me with a parking space that was already vacant.

All that fighting. All that paperwork. For what? For them to give me something they owned all along and were hoarding for the purpose of power. The parking space was vacant, and they still wouldn't assign it to me. That's how ableism works. It uses excessive paperwork to do its dirty work, the work of denying disability accommodations. This apartment was built in a post-ADA world, so these accommodations should have been standard. Yet even in this environment, disabled people must prove our identity with paperwork, federal agency complaints, and housing advocacy before an open space can be ours. Disability doubt is so ingrained, even an empty space cannot be filled without excessive complaint. The ADA is an empty promise, thirty years on.

It's not just snarky DMV employees or apartment complexes with endless paperwork asking me to prove that I deserve disability accommodations. It's the persistent patrolling of my life by complete strangers. I have lost count of the number of times I have been accused of faking my disability. Suspicious strangers, wearing a sly smile, chide me:

Them:	Me:
"You're too young to be disabled."	It's a wheelchair, not whiskey.
"You're too pretty to be disabled."	Thank you, I guess? Eh. Squirm.
"Stop using your grandpa's placard!"	My grandpa's dead, and he's never even been to America.
My personal favorite: "You can't be disabled with a smile like that."	No amount of smiling has ever made my legs work differently.

My disabled body is subjected to interrogation whenever I enter the public sphere. Either from paperwork or from the police, at the grocery store or pumping gas, my body becomes public property. I am surveilled to confirm whether I am performing disability *enough*. And I realize that my white skin, my education, my marriage, and the physical nature of my disability shield me from the worst of it. Disability doubters are exhausting.

"But what about the fakers? They are stealing from the *real* disabled people!" self-proclaimed disability allies whine whenever I raise these concerns. "It's not right that *you* were questioned, but we have to be vigilant to make sure others don't take advantage of the system."

What system? There is no financial or social gain to being disabled, regardless of what TV shows tell you. Roughly 70 percent of disabled people are unemployed, and the majority of those of us who are employed make less than those who aren't disabled.[3] The current system prevents people filing for disability from getting married or owning more than $2,000 in assets, forcing many of us into poverty. Around 60–80 percent of polling places in the US are still inaccessible, even though the law guaranteed us the right to access them over thirty years ago.[4] It is still legal in twenty states to remove children from parental custody simply because a parent is disabled.[5] We do not have the right to parent our own children. We do not have pay parity. We do not have the right to work or vote or enter the public sphere. Why would anyone fake disability? What would they gain?

3. US Bureau of Labor Statistics, "Persons with a Disability: Labor Force Characteristics Summary," news release, February 24, 2021, https://www.bls.gov/news.release/disabl.nr0.htm.

4. United States Government Accountability Office, "Voters with Disabilities: Observations on Polling Place Accessibility and Related Federal Guidance," December 4, 2017, https://www.gao.gov/assets/690/687556.pdf.

5. National Council on Disability, "Rocking the Cradle: Ensuring the Rights of Parents with Disabilities and Their Children," September 27, 2012, https://ncd.gov/publications/2012/Sep272012.

Outside the fictitious fantasy about garnering money and honey from "the system," the problem with this thinking is that it suggests we can discern someone else's disability simply by looking. Disability is not always legible. Some disabilities are external, some are internal. Some are both, depending on the day or the weather. Disability is not always consistent. It can fluctuate from month to month, day to day, or sometimes even hour to hour. Our bodies are not in a fixed state because we are disabled, just as nondisabled bodies experience a range of ability across the span of a year or even a month. Sixty percent of wheelchair users are ambulatory and use wheels for reasons *other* than a permanent inability to walk.[6] Some of us use wheelchairs for pain, fatigue, balance, weakness, or muscle atrophy. This is just one reason why hurling me into a pool *Law & Order*–style proves nothing. Hooray, I can swim! I am still disabled.

Disability is not a monolith. We are the largest marginalized group on earth, made up of a constellation of physicalities and mentalities that shift over time. Since we cannot determine if someone else is disabled simply by looking at them, we should stop trying. There is no upside to doubting strangers' disabilities in the public sphere. Inevitably, these inquisitor visitors harm disabled people more than they detect the small percentage of fakers out there. The fear of the disability con is bigger than the con itself.

Lingering in the invasive questions from these disability doubters is the idea that accommodations are out of altruism and are not based on civil rights. We call this the charity model of disability: it casts disabled people as in constant need of others' generosity. It suggests that disabled people need to be protected, pitied, and patronized.[7]

---

6. Cressida M. R. Hale, "We Need More Awareness of Ambulatory Wheelchair Users," *The Mighty*, November 25, 2018, https://themighty.com/2018/11/ambulatory-wheelchair-users-exist.

7. Mobility International USA, "Models of Disability: An Overview," accessed August 21, 2021, https://www.miusa.org/resource/tipsheet/disabilitymodels.

People think that they are doing something extra, something honorable, something praiseworthy when they treat us as human beings. Ask yourself, would you expect your nondisabled friend to be grateful to be included at church? Or for providing a place for them to pee? Demanding gratitude from disabled people for being included feels like pity. It suggests that disability accommodations are met out of benevolence instead of out of basic civil rights. It sells people the lie that including disabled people is an honorable act of benevolence instead of a faithful act of loving your neighbor. Ableism keeps us grateful.

It's the same thinking that leads churches to host a "special needs" prom instead of providing accommodations that benefit the entire disability community. Sure, it's well-intentioned, but it is based on the notion that if folks are nice enough, we can hold hands, wear matching friendship bracelets, and eventually ableism will disappear. Of course we should be nice to disabled people. But niceness doesn't cure ableism. I shouldn't have to audition for my civil rights.

I have been denied disability parking, educational accommodations, and fair housing. I have been reprimanded by police for parking in my disabled space. I have been ordered to ask permission before bringing my wheelchair to my workplace, as if it is optional. I have been yelled at for requesting accommodations that were signed into law thirty years ago. I have been mocked and cussed out by suspicious strangers accusing me of faking. I have been advised that putting in a (temporary!) ramp at a church isn't "stewarding" tithe money well.

Disabled people are asked to graciously accept the altruism of the community instead of expecting inclusion as part of being fellow humans. It is not benevolent or remarkable to meet someone's federally mandated accommodations. Churches are excluded from this mandate only because many of them fought to keep disabled people out. My disabled license plates, my step-free pass at Disneyland, my parking space are all legal accommodations that should not be considered acts of generosity.

Accusing us of faking disability, using paperwork as an additional hoop that we must jump through, making us prove that we "deserve" our accommodations—all these behaviors suggest that benevolence gave us our civil rights, so spite can withdraw them at any time. It's as if we're given a day pass to enter the nondisabled world, but it can be revoked if we're not grateful enough or don't perform our disability the way we're "supposed" to. As though some of us are more deserving of civil rights than others. There aren't "deserving" or "undeserving" disabled and nondisabled people. There are only image-bearers with a range of abilities and access needs. Our disabilities do not give you the right to treat us as a subcategory of human. My life is worth living, regardless of whether you accommodate me.

I have the right to belong without being pitied. To dream big dreams that aren't someone else's inspiration porn.[8] To go to church without being accosted by people trying to "fix" my body. To be disabled in public without doubters or deniers blocking my path.

I have the right to be reckless. To jump out of planes, dive into the ocean, and take risks. My diagnosis doesn't get to determine the limitations of my life or the lyricism of my limbs.

I have the right to mess up. To talk about my pain without fear that you'll use it against my community later. To not have it all figured out yet. To not be your token.

I have the right to joke about my body. To not share all the invasive details when people ask me what happened and to

---

8. Maysoon Zayid and Stella Young came up with the term "inspiration porn" to describe the way people treat disabled people as inherently inspirational even when we are doing the most mundane tasks. "Porn" deliberately draws on the way this practice objectifies disabled people for nondisabled consumption. We become objects of inspiration rather than subjects with our own stories. To learn more, check out Stella Young, "Inspiration Porn and the Objectification of Disability," TEDx Talks, April 2014, YouTube video, 9:26, https://youtu.be/SxrS7-I_sMQ.

reply, "You should see the *other* guy." To not make my traumatic medical experiences your small talk.

I have the right to be loved. To enter the public space without strangers praising my husband for "putting up with" my disability. To not feel like a burden for having bodily needs.

I have the right to love my disabled body. To celebrate its miraculous ability to prove doctors wrong, time and again. To marvel at how it holds secrets that neurology is still discovering.

I have the right to flourish. To be considered an image-bearer equipped with my own gifts. To be a leader. To use my own voice instead of being a mouthpiece for what you want to say on my behalf. To not have to perform gratitude simply because you include me.

I have the right to be human.

When my appendix burst, they thought it was a stomach bug. "You'd be in more pain if it were anything serious," the doctor chided, making me feel as welcome as hair on a bar of soap. "No," I pleaded between searing jolts, "please run some tests. I know something is wrong." Several impassioned speeches from my husband, two switches in doctors, and fifteen hours later, I was rushed into surgery. After scrubbing out the bacterial debris that had seeped through my abdomen while they were gaslighting me, the surgeons made sure to reprimand me through wide eyes. "Why didn't you tell us you were in this much pain? You could have died!"

But I *had* told them. They just hadn't believed me.

When I first became disabled, I was informed I was faking it for attention. Why someone would want this kind of invasive probing from the medical-industrial complex is beyond me, but here we are. For eighteen months, almost every Tuesday of junior high, I went to the doctor for another test or set of results, chasing the illusive construct of a diagnosis that would offer answers. Diagnosis became a framework for doctors to understand the disorienting experience of my body.[9] To them, I am a case file full of charts, tests, and clinical notes. "Patient is a well-nourished 11-year-old girl," one note reads, as though my food intake is the summation of my preteen life. Every inch of my body has been documented. As the file grows in thickness, it possesses more power over me. At two inches, my file is the proof that something is wrong, but no one can explain what it is. At five inches, the file defends all the opioids, cayenne pepper ointments, and injections cavalierly tested on my limbs. By the time the file fills two cardboard boxes, I am no longer a person with a face or a name; I am a diagnosis, an expert opinion used to garner authority over my true self.

Diagnosis became a justification for increasingly invasive treatments. This is how I wound up in a sterile room in a crispy gown getting stabbed in my spine on repeat, convinced it was good for me. Diagnosis is a way to enforce social control. My body must fit a pre-scripted narrative that the medical-industrial complex can document without me getting in the way. The road to diagnosis for me was paved with three dozen specialists who continuously ordered tests and oscillated between wanting to amputate my leg and claiming it was all in my head. When I was finally diagnosed, the doctor broke the news in embarrassed whispers and patronizing remarks about how I should have told them about the severity of my pain and lack of mobility sooner.

But I *had* told them. They just hadn't believed me.

"If you are silent about your pain, they'll kill you and say you enjoyed it," Zora Neale Hurston taught us.[10] But I wasn't silent about it. They just didn't believe me. Diagnosis is a necessary evil, they claim, because it's the admission ticket to being taken

---

9. For more on the power of diagnosis, check out Eli Clare, *Brilliant Imperfection: Grappling with Cure* (Durham, NC: Duke University Press, 2017), 41.
10. This quotation is generally attributed to Zora Neale Hurston.

seriously by the medical community. Without my hefty boxes of tests and scans, doctors don't believe my embodied experience. Diagnosis is an act of naming what I already told them was true. Diagnosis is a way to get them to believe me.

When people question me about my body, I want to show them my medical files, as if the sheer thickness will make people trust that my disability can't be eaten away with kale or smashed out of my body, hammer-style. I want them to understand I have more medical files than they could ever read. I want them to believe me. But the diagnosis didn't really change any of that, not in any practical way. That's the kicker about being diagnosed with something no one has ever heard of before. Deep down, in the places no one really talks about, some people still don't believe it's real. Not fully, anyway. I am an enigma, a freak, an unknown. On top of the physical aspects of my disability, there's the emotional labor of explaining my body to people who think they get it, but don't. People want to understand something to believe it's real. People try to judge where I fall on the severity scale before they know how to treat me: like DEFCON ratings, but for bodies.

Most people assume that because they have never heard of my disability, it can't be that serious. Whatever they are going through ranks worse. We are not competing for care, for understanding, or for love. It's not Oppression Olympics, but somehow they medal anyway.

Many of these doubts are based on needing to see, to understand, to believe. Turns out not much has changed in the past two thousand years when it comes to disability doubters. When Thomas learns of Jesus's post-resurrection appearance, he questions the women's and disciples' accounts until he sees Jesus for himself. "Unless I see the mark of the nails in his hands, and put my finger in the mark of the nails and my hand in his side, I will not believe," he chimes in, party-pooper style (John 20:25).

Thomas is *all* disability doubters. Not satisfied with the lived experience of his friends, Thomas needs to witness Jesus's wounds for himself. He yearns to see, to touch, to understand, instead of believing his friends' account. He doesn't have all the invasive questions of the DMV or intrusive paperwork of the apartment complex, but he has the same big doubting energy. He wants to make it make sense! But the thing about faith is that it is not always explainable, visible, or understandable.

Disability doubters want to know what my disability is, why they have never heard of it, and how much concern they should show for it. They want my disability to fit into their neat little box of bodies, where there is a set cause and effect for each pang, for every nerve shiver. They want to explain why my body is the way that it is, so they can avoid it happening to them. They want my body to make sense. But the thing about disability is that it is not always explainable, visible, or understandable.

When Thomas doubts, it doesn't seem to be out of malice or cynicism. It's out of wanting certainty. It comes from a place of yearning for things to fit in a pattern that makes sense, complete with guaranteed outcomes and conventional diagnoses. A week later, Jesus appears again, inviting Thomas to "put your finger here and see my hands. Reach out your hand and put it in my side. Do not doubt but believe. . . . Have you believed because you have seen me? Blessed are those who have not seen and yet have come to believe" (John 20:27, 29).

Jesus's body—a scared, disabled body—is the example of the imperishable form, transformed for the glory of God. This disabled body is the exemplar for how our own bodies will be transformed in the eschaton. Thomas seeks to understand what can't be fully explained. He wants to touch the scars and experience the resurrection vicariously. Disability doubters also seek to understand what can't be explained. Perhaps instead of doubting, we should have faith that disability is valid and real. Perhaps instead of rushing to rate disability on a severity scale, we should welcome its disruption to our limited understanding of how bodies function. Perhaps instead of dismissing disability as ugly, we should perceive it as connected to the imperishable body of Christ, whose beautiful, disabling wounds are the marks of our healing.

People are constantly asking me to explain the question mark that is my body, when I don't fully understand it myself most days. *Why* are you disabled? How did this happen? When will you get better? Have you tried ibuprofen (or eucalyptus or heat packs or crystals or snake oil)? People are trying to slot me into their framework of understanding so there can be a tidy reason for me to be this way.

If I showed you my scars, would that make me more human to you? If I paraded my degrees, would that make me more valuable to you? If I performed my trauma, would that make it more real to you? If I told you the name of my diagnosis, would that validate it for you? Does my body need a name for you to include it, learn from it, love it?

My body has a name, but it isn't a disease or a disorder or a disability. It is named "one who wrestles with God," child of the one true King, and woman of valor. That is my one true name, and the only name you need to know.

Blessed are those who don't understand and still welcome my body—scooter, spasms, sporadic symptoms, and all. Blessed are those who do not need to read my mountain of medical records to care for me. Blessed are those who lean not on their own understanding but trust my explanation as valid. Blessed are those who believe me.

REFLECTION AND RESPONSE

▶ Most nondisabled people aren't aware of the ways disabled people must consider accommodations in our everyday experiences. Take this quiz to consider how you access public spaces. For every statement that is true for you, give yourself one point.

1. Strangers do not typically ask what's wrong with me.
2. I can generally sit with my friends when I attend a concert or performance.
3. When I go out to eat or shop, I trust there will be a public bathroom I can use.
4. I can ride in cars, in rideshares, or on public transportation without worrying if they will accommodate my body.
5. I am protected by minimum wage laws.
6. When I dine out, waiters ask me (and not my companions) what I would like to order.
7. I can find housing that meets my physical needs.
8. Strangers do not typically offer medical advice to me.
9. Random people do not tell me that my body is caused by sin.
10. My daily cost of living is about the same as everyone else's.
11. At my workplace, I am assured that there is a plan for my escape in the event of a fire.
12. I can get married without worrying about losing my income.
13. I am not typically told people would rather be dead than live in my body.
14. Usually, people do not mock the way I walk or talk.
15. People do not ask to play with my limbs or accessories.

▶ Reflect on your experience of taking this quiz. How many "points" do you have? Post your score at MyBodyIsNotA PrayerRequest.com. Have you ever considered these concerns before taking this quiz? How has your experience of public space shaped your understanding of what is "normal" and "natural" when it comes to bodies? If any of these concerns are a surprise to you, let that be an invitation to you to learn more about the experiences of disabled people and the lack of accommodations for us in public spaces.

▸ Read the #AbleismExists and #EverydayAbleism hashtags on Twitter to learn from other disabled people about their experiences of everyday ableism. Consider whether there is anything you can commit to changing in your own language, behavior, or etiquette after learning from the expertise of disabled people.

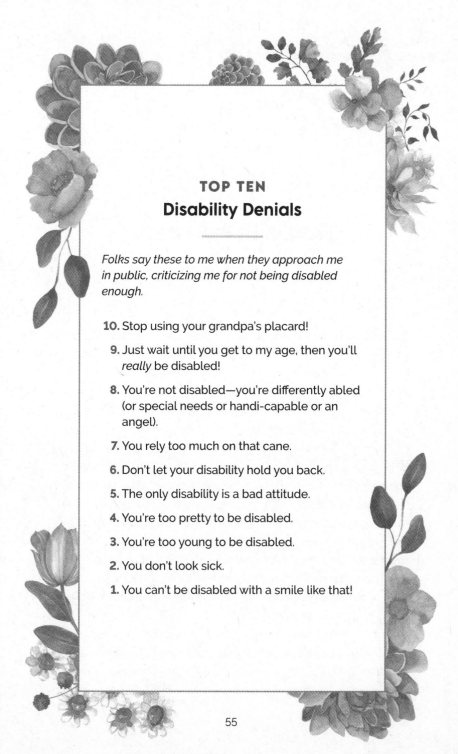

TOP TEN
Disability Denials

Folks say these to me when they approach me in public, criticizing me for not being disabled enough.

10. Stop using your grandpa's placard!

9. Just wait until you get to my age, then you'll *really* be disabled!

8. You're not disabled—you're differently abled (or special needs or handi-capable or an angel).

7. You rely too much on that cane.

6. Don't let your disability hold you back.

5. The only disability is a bad attitude.

4. You're too pretty to be disabled.

3. You're too young to be disabled.

2. You don't look sick.

1. You can't be disabled with a smile like that!

Disability Justice

His cold, wrinkled hands inspect my body like a Ferrari he's admiring. He takes in each muscle, every scar, like he's consuming my V8 engine with his greedy eyes. I am not even human to his stethoscope, but a series of diagnostics awaiting his magical touch. Every time I answer his demands, he interjects, making sure I realize my opinion isn't relevant to my own medical care. Only *his* view of my prognosis matters. When I ask the rationale behind ordering another round of tests—MRI, CT scan, basic metabolic panel, and nerve conduction velocity tests among them—he says that's not my concern. His greedy mitts on my pelvis now, he examines my hip flexor. Prickly pangs reverberate through my torso as he puppets the movement of my calf, examining the range of motion of my hip. In an alternate timeline, I slap his hands and kick him away with a jolt as "Don't Stop Me Now" booms in the background of my epic takedown sequence.

But I waited months to land a coveted appointment with this double board-certified neurosurgeon, and I need his autograph to order my experimental medication. I draw an invisible barrier with my eyes, telling myself that if his hands intrude beyond that point, I will slap him away in *this* timeline, Queen soundtrack or not. He and one of the other surgeons talk about me as though I am not in the room. "She might respond to an intrathecal drug pump," they concur without my input. My body is the lab for their experiment. I interrupt the speculation about my sympathetic nervous system and am informed that I've "rejected the medical community" by not trusting their advice without question. I don't need to know what the tests are for. As I make my way out, they thrust a bill for $300 in my face with a strict warning not to ask so many irritating questions next time. "You're a nosy one, aren't you?" the famous surgeon says with a wink as I leave, his unwelcome hand squeezing my shoulder. It doesn't take my nose to know his bedside manner stinks.

Most doctors don't want me to be human. They prefer diseases, diagnoses, and drugs. They want me to be a silent medical chart in their examination process, never asking why or how, never divulging the pain or the effect their instructions have on my life. So long as I follow directions, present a textbook disease to them, and remove all humanity from the appointment, they allow me to attend. They think the alphabet soup behind their names justifies jeering at my questions.

Many churches are just like these doctors. They want me to perform the role of a suffering or pious disabled person, depending on how much Calvin they've internalized. So long as I am gazing up into the distant stars, longing for a time when I am released from this mortal torment, they understand how to treat me. Doctors have drugs, churches have platitudes. They use platitudes like a drug they can dole out to make any ailment go away. I become the saintly disabled person, silently suffering, waiting for the sweet release of death. Insert halo here. Whenever I say I'm doing well, they scorn me. Whenever I ask why they are uncomfortable with embracing disability, they tell me I have "given up hope." Many churches have doused Jesus's healing in a white coat and a prescription pad for platitudes, pretending it's the gospel. They even mimic the doctors' arrogance whenever questioned. They think they know best. The only difference between doctors endorsing procedures and churches sanctioning platitudes is a medical degree.

"Your body is a result of the fall," this pastor says, as though he's trying to hang up the phone with a telemarketer. "If you had a little more faith, you wouldn't have to live under the curse of the fall." Fear and avoidance loiter in his words, with the weight of conveying something heavy to a child.

Fall-mongers are sure to emphasize that my body is "a result of the fall," but they don't recall that God promises to make the lame a remnant for new creation. They forget that God, when speaking to Moses, takes credit for making people "mute or deaf, seeing or blind" when they dismiss my disability (Exod. 4:11). They are too busy giving me poems entitled "No Wheelchairs in Heaven" to reflect on why that makes them rejoice. (This is an actual poem I have received on multiple occasions from relative strangers.)

Trying to explain my existence to them is exhausting, particularly because even within their theological framework, it doesn't make sense. Everyone currently alive is implicated by the fall. Disabled bodies carry the weight of being labeled "products of the fall," as if all bodies are not implicated in the cosmic tyrannies of sin and suffering. Clothing is also a result of the fall, but I have never learned of anyone shaming clothing stores or weeping at a lyric that proclaims, "no more jeans in heaven because we'll finally be healed and whole!" The fall has become a convenient way to distance the beloved community from disabled people. We become scapegoats, with people rushing up to cure us, hoisting the world's problems onto our bodies instead of asking tough questions about how they participate in a system that keeps our bodies down. We represent people's worst fears. To many, we bear the marks of judgment, decay, or disease. But, in reality, we display the prophetic witness of what is true for all humans. All bodies are interdependent and fragile; ours just make it more evident. All humans bear the image of God; that doesn't diminish after the fall—or even after *a* fall that results in a disability.

The prophetic witness of the disability community is that we reveal what will likely become true about all humans over time. Disability theologian Thomas Reynolds even goes as far as to suggest that we should privilege disability as the norm to reverse the "cult of normalcy."[1] Maybe then the broader world would learn what our disabled bodies declare to be true. Our lives, our body-minds puncture the illusion of "normalcy" and invite us to dismantle the idols of prosperity, productivity, and independence. Disabled people bear an unfair burden for what is true about all of humanity; temporarily nondisabled people just don't realize it yet. Our bodies are not self-sufficient. We cannot rely solely on ourselves. We must become interdependent to thrive. We must learn to promote disability justice to help restore coflourishing among humanity.

Disability justice affirms the unique qualities and knowledge of each body-mind. It stresses that no body—disabled or otherwise—is inherently worth more than another. Each body has needs and strengths that fluctuate over time. Disability justice doesn't create a hierarchy of needs but holds that all bodies have needs that must be met without shame. The disability justice movement is built on the premise that all bodies must move together to thrive, so that no person is left behind.[2] It moves at the pace of the most vulnerable, most marginalized, so that everyone can thrive.

1. Thomas E. Reynolds, *Vulnerable Communion: A Theology of Disability and Hospitality* (Grand Rapids: Brazos, 2008), 104.
2. Sins Invalid, *Skin, Tooth, and Bone: The Basis of Our Movement Is Our People; A Disability Justice Primer*, 2nd ed. (Berkeley: Sins Invalid, 2019), 10–14.

Disability justice is a lot like the description of the goodness between the community of creation. Churches too quickly start the story with the forbidden fruit—when everything went wrong. But the story begins before humans order the wrong thing off the Eden menu. In Genesis 1, humans are made in the image of God and bear God's image to the world. Yes, even your annoying coworker who overshares and your uncle who picks on you at the family potluck. All humans bear God's image, including us disabled ones.

Genesis 1:31 notes that everything God made was "very good." In *The Very Good Gospel*, prophet Lisa Sharon Harper explains the connotation of "very good" in the original text: "The Greeks located perfection within the object itself. A thing or a person strove toward perfection. But the Hebrews understood goodness to be located *between* things. As a result, the original hearers would have understood *tov* to refer to the goodness of the ties and relationships between things in creation."[3]

The Greeks erected statues showcasing the elite qualities of their heroes, like marble versions of Instagram influencers. Hero-worship, much? They perceived goodness in the thing itself: the muscular thighs, the "ideal" proportions, and the burly arms. But God didn't imprint the divine image on an elect few with chiseled abs and sturdy jaw lines. And Genesis doesn't talk about pre-fall humanity as perfect, nondisabled athletes with the strength and agility of Simone Biles. We *all* have God's image—regardless of how smart we are, how much we "contribute to society," how our bodies function, or what we believe. Isn't that liberating? Because, frankly, who can live up to the wonder that is Simone Biles? There is nothing you can achieve or mess up that can take God's image away from you. You don't have to earn it or prove that you are worth it.

3. Lisa Sharon Harper, *The Very Good Gospel: How Everything Wrong Can Be Made Right* (Colorado Springs: WaterBrook, 2016), 30.

It is intrinsic to your being. That means we are not striving to become better versions of ourselves. We are all invited to participate in cultivating the goodness God intended between humans, animals, and the earth, instead of focusing on "bettering" ourselves. We are invested in one another's flourishing.

Creation being "very good" is not about achieving individual perfection to better ourselves through the Enneagram or essential oils. We can read Scripture every day or self-help all we like, but that's not how Scripture defines the goodness God created. Which, for a recovering perfectionist, is a real bummer. We are so good at striving to perform our worth! We think if we reach the mythical goal of perfection, we will be beyond vulnerability. But the space between us matters more to our understanding of the goodness God created. Goodness happens when the betweenness is restored. Without supporting our neighbor's flourishing, we are missing out on the vehement goodness of creation. We are limiting the goodness between us.

If we really believed the good news that we claim to cherish, we would find ourselves advocating for disability justice as part of our role as fellow image-bearers. Disabled people bear God's image. Not despite our bodies or once we receive our "new-creation bodies." Right now, disabled people in wheelchairs, using their ventilators, and communicating in diverse ways radiate God's image to the world. We are just waiting for the rest of the world to realize this and help create that vibrant goodness between disabled and nondisabled neighbors. The vibrant goodness between me and fellow churchgoers was broken when prayerful perpetrators accosted me without knowing anything about me. The vibrant goodness was broken when I was informed that my disability is a result of my sin. The vibrant goodness was broken when I was dismissed for asking people to change their ableist language. The vibrant goodness was broken when my body, and my body alone, was blamed for the fall of all humanity.

The good news is that the story does not stop there. We can restore the vibrant, abundant, radical goodness between me and fellow churchgoers by caring about disability justice. We can choose to help cocreate our neighbor's flourishing. We are not seeking to fix our neighbor's physical impairment, but to generate a world that does not encumber our neighbor for that impairment. Our flourishing is connected. Your flourishing is linked to disability justice, whether you realize it or not. To advocate for disability justice is simply to recognize the *imago Dei* in every body-mind, regardless of ability, aptitude, and appearance.

If I had known what I would find in my inbox when I hit the blue icon, I wouldn't have checked my email that windy Monday morning, less than ten minutes before I had to go to a meeting. Scrolling through my catalog of emails, my eyes barely graze over the litany of ads, recommended products, and junk mail before hitting delete. And then I see it. The email I've been waiting for.

I click on it without thinking, without blinking, without carbon dioxide escaping my clenched jaw. My eyes are immediately sucked in to the bold, condemning letters at the bottom: "You owe $1,624.97." The numbers wring out my lungs like a sponge. One thousand, six hundred twenty-four dollars and ninety-seven cents, for a procedure I am supposed to have every three weeks. The numbers swirl in my mind like that GIF of "math lady" mentally calculating complex equations inside her head. Quick arithmetic tells me I will rack up $20,000 before the year ends. And that's *after* insurance—just for these procedures. Somehow this isn't what I had in mind when I learned I was "bought with a price" (1 Cor. 6:20). That amount doesn't tally the total for physical therapies, medications, and any other medical expenses that might emerge along the way. I add it to the stack of medical bills flooding my inbox and force myself to exhale, rushing off to a meeting that I attend as a shadow of myself.

Sometimes I think about all the money that has been spent on my body. Piles of gold, enough to buy a Lamborghini or a vacation house. I don't want either of those status symbols, but when I am too fatigued to sleep, I picture Scrooge McDuck diving into the money vault full of gold coins to pay for my medical care. Do the gold coins have a lubricant we don't know about, I wonder? Surely plunging into a pit of gold coins would break McDuck's neck upon impact. As would swimming under the crushing weight of gold. Luckily, this duck-billed gold-digger could afford the crip tax to pay all his medical bills.

Crip tax is a term for the way society charges disabled people for being disabled. The cost of mobility devices, medical care, and assistive technology is weighty. One study found that disabled adults in the United States pay an extra $10,000–$30,000 just for being disabled—per year. Every year. That's not even including the portion covered by health insurance.[4] Being disabled is expensive. The world charges us an additional price of admission.

Imagine if instead of trying to pray away my body, Christian communities invested in making sure they didn't bankrupt me. Imagine if churches ensured that no disabled person in their community paid the crip tax alone. Imagine if we were invested in one another's thriving enough to pick up the bill. Perhaps then the vibrant goodness could be restored between us. For nondisabled people to pay the crip tax affirms that we are not a burden. It's a way to undo the systems that keep disabled people down. It declares that we do not have to pay for

4. Sophie Mitra et al., "Extra Costs of Living with a Disability: A Review and Agenda for Research," *Disability and Health Journal* 10, no. 4 (2017): 475–84, https://doi.org /10.1016/j.dhjo.2017.04.007.

the consequences of an inaccessible society all by ourselves. It shows us that our nondisabled neighbors realize our thriving is dependent on one another, and that they take disability justice seriously. It proves that you really do understand that you have been #blessed.

Churches can move beyond focusing on including disabled people and instead invest in our thriving through mutuality, not impersonal charity. One way to do this is by sharing the crip tax with disabled people in your community, but there are so many additional ways to ensure that your disabled neighbors flourish. I have experienced glimpses of a community committed to healing and interdependence over curing and independence. When I was in high school, my leg was blue from the lack of blood circulation and my hair stopped growing. There was talk of amputation. In physical therapy, they had us set goals to judge our progress. Mine was that I'd be able to wear socks. Shoes were a thing of the past. I learned terms like "hallucinogenic" and "Drug Enforcement Administration" before I knew how to drive. When other teens were thinking about college applications and prom, I was generally to be found doing homework on the road, trying to write steadily despite the freeway potholes on the way to one of my various medical appointments, three times a week with specialists who were forty miles away because few doctors know how to treat my rare body. Our church rallied around me and my family and took turns driving me so my parents didn't have to do it alone. That's what restoring the vibrant goodness between us looks like. That's coflourishing. That's healing. It's being part of a community that meets you where you are—even on the freeway on the way to the doctor—and helps fulfill your needs instead of trying to fix you and ditch you. It's recognizing that, in the beloved community, one person's struggle is everyone's struggle.

Restoring the vibrant goodness between us looks like me coaching parents on how to talk to their kids about disability.

Because I am disabled, my body speaks a language that is foreign to most nondisabled parents, so I have become a translator, helping parents and kids understand one another and easing the tension of isolation that exists within families. Being disabled doesn't always come with parents who are disabled, so it can be an isolating experience. Even the most loving and attentive parents have a lot to learn and unlearn (ahem, ableism) when it comes to supporting their disabled child. Restoring the vibrant goodness between us looks like sitting with one of my disabled mentees in her frustration because no one else in her life understands the toll that daily ableist microaggressions take on her. Restoring the vibrant goodness between us looks like my husband helping me put on my shoes or carrying me up the stairs without ever making me feel like a burden. Restoring the vibrant goodness between us looks like people treating me as a capable human, not a scary diagnosis in need of eradication.

When we approach life with a healing mindset instead of a curing mindset, we invest in the flourishing of our neighbors and open ourselves up to all kinds of possibilities that we never thought possible. My story, my disability, my healing has a ripple effect in the community. It is not just my body that benefits from the knowledge of healing; it is good news for the whole community. It allows others to reimagine what flourishing can be. When we are deeply invested in one another's lives, there is no limit to how the healing of disability justice can flow throughout the community. Coflourishing is enduring, messy work, but when we do it, it is very, very good. It's almost like God intended it that way.

REFLECTION AND RESPONSE

▶ Create a community care network in your community to meet the needs of disabled people. Ask disabled people what their material needs are: bring dinner, walk their dog, or clean the toilets for your disabled friends. A garage sale or car wash can raise money to pay the crip tax for someone in your community. Community care should be proactive, specific to the needs of the individual, and always done with companionship and collaboration, never pity.

▶ The Accessible Icon (https://accessibleicon.org) is in the public domain, is free to use, and promotes a more active, engaged, and empowered disabled person (compared to the passive, stagnant figure typically depicted on signs). Consider using this icon in your church, city, or community. The icon is part of design activism, a way to generate conversation around the way disabled people are portrayed in the public space.

▶ Rewrite narratives about disability that are harmful. The poem "No Wheelchairs in Heaven" by J. Morse has been given to me by strangers (or near strangers) several times. I reimagine this poem as "No Stares in Heaven" because I will no longer be mocked "in a wheelchair . . . and loaded down with" cruel stares. Practice rewriting narratives to allow disability to be more than a metaphor or a faking trope.

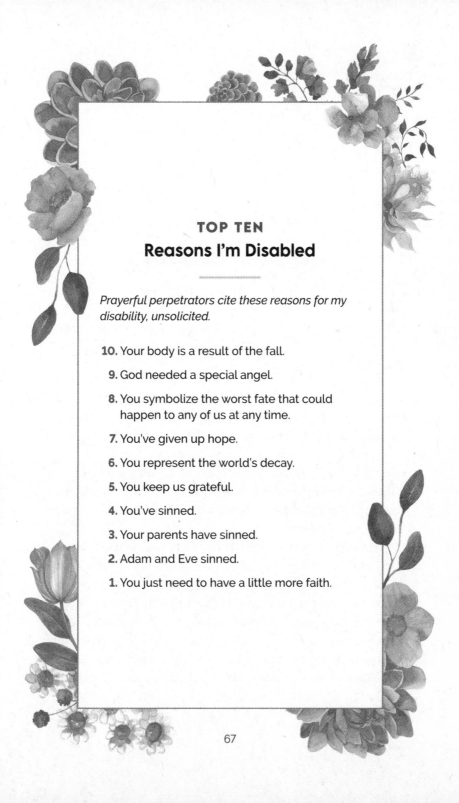

TOP TEN
Reasons I'm Disabled

Prayerful perpetrators cite these reasons for my disability, unsolicited.

10. Your body is a result of the fall.

9. God needed a special angel.

8. You symbolize the worst fate that could happen to any of us at any time.

7. You've given up hope.

6. You represent the world's decay.

5. You keep us grateful.

4. You've sinned.

3. Your parents have sinned.

2. Adam and Eve sinned.

1. You just need to have a little more faith.

Disability Blessings

I sing Destiny's Child's "Survivor" while it happens. Not aloud—as much as I dislike these doctors, I don't want to torture them, especially not while they are puncturing my spine. No, I sing in my head, hoping the lyrics will convince me that I can actually survive this. By the time I get to "you thought that I'd be helpless without you but I'm smarter," I am already through the local anesthetic and steroid injections. The fluoroscopy dye goes in with "wishin' you the best, pray that you are blessed" and the medicine when Michelle starts singing the second bridge.[1]

The nurse cautioned me that I wouldn't be able to tolerate watching the syringes pierce my skin, that I needed to let the doctors do their jobs without "getting in the way." I remember my friend's joke about consent: that I could run over a guy's foot with my scooter if he tried to make me do anything I don't want to. I want to witness what is done to my body, even if only voyeuristically. So I bring my own mirror and remain motionless while they shove the surgical instruments five inches into my

1. "Survivor," on Destiny's Child, *Survivor*, Columbia, 2001.

curved spine. I've been doing this for weeks, yet somehow the doctor remains shocked that I am tranquil while watching him work behind my back with the magic of the mirror. By age, I am fifteen; by medical procedures, I am geriatric.

Frigid, I lie perfectly still for twenty minutes after stern warnings that if I move, I might become paralyzed. I already can't walk, so these threats don't carry the weight the surgeon believes. But he's made more than one misogynistic comment about how little pain "teenage girls" can handle, so I am determined to prove him wrong. I don't back down from a challenge, particularly when carrying the reputation of all girls. I do not flinch until they collect my body to wheel me outside. Me, a prop in their chronicle about cure. Sleepy, stiff, and sore, I go home to vomit.

After doing this every Thursday for a year, I finally refuse to go back. Turns out I don't need to run over anyone's foot to withdraw consent. All their cautions about long-term effects and pleas to give it more time are lost on me. Sure, I'm a survivor, but what if I don't have to be? Maybe I could stop wrestling with my body and finally accept that I am disabled.

"You'll regret this," the doctor spits out. He warns my parents they shouldn't leave medical decision-making to a sixteen-year-old girl. After all, it's only my body that is gouged in these procedures. *They* are the ones who sign over consent. To him, anything—even vomiting all night after being repeatedly stabbed in the spine—is better than using a wheelchair. *Anything* is worth walking.

It's difficult for nondisabled people to understand how I would rather be disabled than a lab rat. "Isn't it worth it if it gets you walking, even just for a day?" Their doe eyes try to convince me. My body has been poked and prodded in ways that nondisabled people could never imagine. At first it was cayenne pepper ointments to rub on my leg. All they did was make me hungry for a vindaloo curry. Next came the injections of corticosteroids and opioids. Too many drugs to recall, the only trace of them the craters they burned in my intestinal tract. I took hallucinogens before I was old enough to fully understand what they were. My parents explained them to me through the litmus test of our German shepherd, Rusty, flying. If I saw Rusty flying, they warned me, then I was hallucinating. In jest, my dad would even carry Rusty throughout the house to make it seem as though she were soaring, fur flapping in the breeze. "Have you had any hallucinations lately, darl?" he'd inquire with a knowing smirk.

You name it, I've tried it: cupping, electromyographic biofeedback, Pilates, hypnotherapy, acupuncture, osteopathic manipulation, transcutaneous electrical nerve stimulation, epidural steroid injections, chiropractic management, bioelectric therapy, neural blockages, sports massage therapy, mirror therapy, yoga, glial cell modulation, neuroplasticity training, and a catalog of other wacky methods the medical community convinced me would work with false hope and hefty price tags. I've gone to physical therapy so much that the main therapist jokes I've logged more hours than the residents. I spent more time with my medical team than with friends in high school.

I have been x-rayed, radio-rayed, and gamma rayed. Radioactive particles have been injected into my veins. I came away without superhero powers, despite what all Marvel origin stories led me to believe. I have been placed inside magnetic tubes with cacophonous clanking charting my organs and tissues. Not even my insides are shrouded from the invasive gaze of the medical-industrial complex. No space on my body is safe from them. I have been thrown into a pool with my legs bound, weights strapped to my limbs, all while being coached that pain is *good* for me. "It's worth it," they promise behind stopwatches and clipboards. I have been tied to machines and forced to climb over hurdles (not a metaphor) to counteract muscle atrophy. "Use it or lose it!" they joke.

All these treatments were done *to* me, and came with empty promises of walking or running (gasp!) in the near future. If we just get through the "adjustment" phase, we'll notice a difference, the white coats guarantee, without considering the physical impact of that phase. "Quality of life" is a phrase that is thrown around a lot. Replica hope is the drug they deal. The problem with these increasingly invasive procedures is that they are all based on a medical model of disability, one that assumes we must go to extreme lengths to fix the problem of my body. The medical model casts the individual as the problem. It proclaims that one body is out of sync with the rest of humanity and therefore must be stabbed and jabbed for as long as it takes to produce results. Make no mistake, it takes forever. The medical model believes that disability is inherently tragic and must be avoided at all costs, up to and including tens of thousands of dollars a year and amplified agony. But hey, if you are unlucky enough to be disabled, you can suffer through endless medical procedures on the boulevard of broken ableist dreams. The assumption is that disabled people live miserable lives anyway, so subjecting us to aggressive procedures is my penance.[2] Whatever it takes for a greater race of humans.

To be sure, there are medical issues that we should treat, and many disabled people can and do use a range of medical practices to address specific aspects of living with their disability. In my case, the problem was that the medical community recommended increasingly drastic measures to try to "overcome" disability instead of using medicine to support my disabled body. Situating disability only in a medical framework inevitably produces medical solutions instead of a mix of medical and social responses. I wish one doctor—just one out of the dozens and dozens of specialists I have been treated by—had mustered the courage to suggest embracing disability instead of trying to erase it. I wish my teenage self could have met cool crips who are empowered and fierce not despite their bodies, but because of them.

2. One study found that 80 percent of doctors report that disabled people have a worse quality of life. Anita Slomski, "Doctors Share Views on Patients with Disability," *Harvard Gazette*, February 1, 2021, https://news.harvard.edu/gazette/story/2021/02/survey-finds-doctors-have-negative-perception-of-patients-with-disability.

I wish I wasn't sold the lie that an amputated leg or a wheelchair is the worst fate that can happen, worse than death. Perhaps then I wouldn't have been physically tortured for so long. Perhaps then I would have embraced that I'm disabled a lot sooner.

Most narratives about disability are inherently negative. Comic book villains from Ulysses Klaue (*Black Panther*) to Mr. Glass (*Unbreakable*) to Dr. Poison and Ares/Sir Patrick Morgan (*Wonder Woman*) teach us that superheroes are *not* the ones with disabilities. Even Darth Vader's descent to the Dark Side coincides with his disfigurement. Disability is to be feared, ostracized, and villainized. It becomes an external manifestation of some inner malevolence. Ultimately, the hero defeats the character with the disability and restores normative order to the world. Insert collective sigh of relief. Everyone left is nondisabled and therefore "moral." Doctors, well-intentioned though they may be, are not immune to these narratives. Nor are churches.

When we finally receive a portrayal of disability that is *not* conflated with evil, it is generally depicted by a nondisabled actor putting on disability like a costume for an Academy Award.[3] (Looking at you, Eddie Redmayne.[4]) In fact, the quickest way to secure an Oscar nod is by playing a disabled character, as if our bodies are props that can be used for accolades but quickly discarded when they become too heavy, too spontaneous, or too

3. Portrayals of disability are only 2 percent of the roles, despite being 25 percent of the population. Only 5 percent of these limited roles are played by someone who is disabled, yet playing such a role greatly increases the nondisabled person's chances of garnering critical acclaim and awards. Danny Woodburn and Kristina Kopić, "The Ruderman White Paper on Employment of Actors with Disabilities in Television," Ruderman Family Foundation, July 2016, https://www.rudermanfoundation.org/wp-content /uploads/2016/07/TV-White-Paper_7-1-003.pdf.

4. When Eddie Redmayne won an Oscar for his portrayal of Stephen Hawking in *The Theory of Everything* in 2014, more than half of Academy Awards best actor nominations were for portrayals of disabled characters by nondisabled actors.

messy. Disability cannot be reconstructed via empathy cosplay. You can't use a wheelchair for an afternoon and understand what my life is like. Most people's experiences of disabled people are cartoonish caricatures, with nondisabled actors putting our physicality on like a costume. "That's called acting," you might counter. But this practice has been linked to underdiagnosing certain disabilities that do not present in the "stereotypical" way illustrated on film.[5] Acting relies on performing disability in a way that is recognizable to the nondisabled gaze. Narratives construct reality around other characters' experiences of the disabled person instead of giving humanity to the disabled character. This leads to real-world consequences for disabled people, who are underdiagnosed, dismissed, or doubted for not being "disabled enough" by the medical system and random strangers (hello, DMV!) we encounter in everyday life.

Ableism is so pervasive in the stories our society tells about disability that audiences believe them without inquiring whether they are even true. Disabled characters are metaphors and little else. They are repositories for nondisabled fears about becoming disabled. They do not possess multifaceted personalities that exist in the real world. Generally, there are two acceptable roles for disabled characters in movies, pop culture, and society:

1. **Archetype:** Villainous disabled nemesis

   Qualities: Melancholic angst, dejected resentment—he's got an axe to grind with the world because of his unfair lot in life (read: he's disabled, after all!).

   Catchphrase: "Let the hate flow through you" or "I'm not a monster. I'm just ahead of the curve."[6]

5. Sarah Bradley, "TV Is Obsessed with an Unrealistic Portrayal of Autistic People," *Vice*, October 25, 2017, https://www.vice.com/en/article/j5j8zb/tv-is-obsessed-with-unrealistic-portrayal-of-autistic-people.

6. The first quotation is from Emperor Palpatine in *Return of the Jedi* (1983). The second is from the Joker in *The Dark Knight* (2008).

Purpose: Disability acts as both cause and symptom of his comic-book villainy, but it doesn't need to be explained because everyone assumes he is angry at the world. His disability is usually acquired, so it can serve as the only juicy detail given from his tragic backstory.

2. **Archetype:** Virtuous disabled overcomer (a.k.a. supercrip)[7]

Qualities: Abundant patience, winsome attitude, saccharine smile.

Catchphrase: "Everything happens for a reason" or "the only disability is a bad attitude."

Purpose: She'll serve as your inspiration so you can overcome the difficulty of your sprained ankle or overdemanding boss. She inspires you to do everything with a smile, because she's the epitome of the person who has it "worse off." Her personality is almost entirely undetectable, except when you need someone to remind you that at least you're not disabled.

These disabled characters become empty receptacles on which nondisabled writers project their pity, as though disabled people are objects of suffering instead of subjects with unique personalities and spiritual gifts. Disability must always serve a loftier "purpose" that drives narrative closure instead of simply existing as part of bodily diversity. Most narratives teach us that disabled characters demand narrative termination. Cure them—or kill them off.[8] As if all we needed was an emboldening "Run, Forrest, run!" or a revenge plot to cast off our coma-induced disability

---

7. Joseph P. Shapiro, *No Pity: People with Disabilities Forging a New Civil Rights Movement* (New York: Times Books, 1994), 16.

8. For more on this narrative practice, check out David T. Mitchell and Sharon L. Snyder, *Narrative Prosthesis: Disability and the Dependencies of Discourse* (Ann Arbor: University of Michigan Press, 2000).

and escape to freedom.[9] Just try really hard and you, too, can wiggle your toes. (Yes, I've been told that before, in case you were wondering.) Disability has already served its function and therefore can be discarded. Phew! No need for the audience to experience the discomfort of an "unresolved" or meaningless disability. The roles for disabled people are pre-scripted to ensure that nondisabled people feel noble about themselves, as if our entire existence is in service to their emotional journeys.

When the medical-industrial complex couldn't cure me, the narrative switched to overcoming instead. Overcoming is the backup plan.[10] It places the onus on me to do the work of erasing disability from the discourse, ensuring that no one must behold my twisted physicality for too long. People don't feel as uncomfortable with my disability when they focus on how I love to read or hang out with friends experiencing homelessness at the local laundromat. I am not so much a person as an idea: a supercrip who overcomes a disability through sheer determination and will. The focus on personal determination instead of social change is convenient for people who do not wish to change.

To live with a disability, then, is to live a life of erasure. There is no space for us to live fully embodied lives outside of offering inspiration porn.[11] Sure, we are box office gold when we "overcome" our physical limitations or maintain an optimistic attitude while surviving a diagnosis that everyone openly dreads. No wonder I spent so much time trying to outpace being disabled. Overcoming is the messaging we all receive!

9. I reference *Forrest Gump* and *Kill Bill* here, but "throwing off a disability" is a well-documented trope. "Throwing Off the Disability," TV Tropes, accessed September 8, 2021, https://tvtropes.org/pmwiki/pmwiki.php/Main/ThrowingOffTheDisability.

10. Eli Clare, *Brilliant Imperfection: Grappling with Cure* (Durham, NC: Duke University Press, 2017), 10.

11. Maysoon Zayid and Stella Young came up with the term "inspiration porn." Check out Stella Young, "Inspiration Porn and the Objectification of Disability," TEDx Talks, April 2014, YouTube video, 9:26, https://youtu.be/SxrS7-I_sMQ.

The hubris of strangers offering remedies to cure my disability derives from these reductive kill-or-cure narratives. I am not a character in *that* story. I do not get to throw off my disability in a poignant crescendo to make audiences feel better about themselves. There is no available narrative that fits my disability. It is visible and invisible, public and private, existing in the liminal space of crip time.[12] When I am walking, my disability lurks beneath like muscle memory of another life. I know what it's like to experience the world from below, sitting in my wheelchair. When I use my mobility scooter, I know the movements that my legs can no longer make. *Heel, toe, heel, toe, heel, toe.* My body keeps score even when no one else registers my disability. My body exists in no narrative because it is complex, nuanced, and messy, and it does not offer neat resolution. My disability is dynamic.[13]

It should come as no surprise that we use these disability archetypes when interpreting Scripture. We read healing narratives as eradicating disability (curing) without considering the broader social implications (healing). We omit the disabilities of Moses, Jesus, and Paul when telling their stories. We are surprised to learn that scholars think Zacchaeus was a little person because we have completely omitted disability from our sanctified imaginations.[14] We equate sin with disability despite Jesus telling us otherwise. Yet disability is not always cured or

---

12. For more on crip time, check out Ellen Samuels's article "Six Ways of Looking at Crip Time," *Disability Studies* 37, no. 3 (2017), https://dsq-sds.org/article/view/5824/4684.

13. For more on this idea, check out Brianne Benness, "My Disability Is Dynamic," *Medium*, December 8, 2019, https://medium.com/age-of-awareness/my-disability-is-dynamic-bc2a619fcc1.

14. Amos Yong, "Zacchaeus: Short and Un-seen," *Christian Reflection: Disability* (2012): 11–17, https://www.baylor.edu/content/services/document.php/188193.pdf.

killed off in Scripture. Disability acts as a blessing, a revelation, and a prophetic witness to the community. It even becomes a mark of the covenant for Jacob, who becomes disabled at a crucial phase of the narrative. His disability acts as the catalyst for radical transformation.

Jacob's story of becoming disabled is a weird one. You might remember that Jacob and his twin brother Esau don't get along very well. Perhaps it has something to do with the fact that Jacob beguiles Esau into giving up his birthright—which is his extra inheritance as the firstborn—in exchange for a measly bowl of lentil stew. Of all the things to trade your birthright for, this seems like a bit of a letdown. What a lentil loss. Or it might have to do with the fact that Jacob is a mama's boy. Or maybe it's because Jacob tricks their dad, Isaac, into giving him Esau's blessing. Slyly, he dons goatskin to commit the charade. He is not the GOAT.

Esau promises to kill Jacob in response to all this deceit and trickery. And frankly, who can blame him? This makes most of our sibling rivalries look tame and uninspired. So Jacob figures he'll wait out Esau's anger at their uncle Laban's house. Twenty years, two wives, and eleven sons later, he's on his way back to Canaan when we meet up with him in Genesis 32:

> During the night Jacob got up and took his two wives, his two servant wives, and his eleven sons and crossed the Jabbok River with them. After taking them to the other side, he sent over all his possessions.
> This left Jacob all alone in the camp, and a man came and wrestled with him until the dawn began to break. When the man saw that he would not win the match, he touched Jacob's hip and wrenched it out of its socket. Then the man said, "Let me go, for the dawn is breaking!"
> But Jacob said, "I will not let you go unless you bless me."
> "What is your name?" the man asked.
> He replied, "Jacob."

"Your name will no longer be Jacob," the man told him. "From now on you will be called Israel, because you have fought with God and with men and have won."

"Please tell me your name," Jacob said.

"Why do you want to know my name?" the man replied. Then he blessed Jacob there.

Jacob named the place Peniel (which means "face of God"), for he said, "I have seen God face to face, yet my life has been spared." The sun was rising as Jacob left Peniel, and he was limping because of the injury to his hip. (Even today the people of Israel don't eat the tendon near the hip socket because of what happened that night when the man strained the tendon of Jacob's hip.) (Gen. 32:22–32 NLT)

Admittedly, this is a wild passage. A wrestling angel who wrenches Jacob's hip out doesn't exactly make for "flannel board" material for Sunday school. But this passage can teach us a great deal about how disability becomes a blessing and a mark of a covenant relationship with God. Two changes occur here—the name change and the physical change—and both are signs of God's blessing to Jacob and marks of the covenant.

Names don't carry the same consequence to us today as they once did. I'm historically horrible with names. That's not false modesty. Names don't adhere to my mental space. My brain is Teflon. That was a pleasant surprise about life switching to Zoom during the pandemic. Names were clearly displayed, saving me the embarrassment of not knowing what to call work proximity associates that I've introduced myself to one too many times. But names in antiquity connected people to their lineage and gave them a reputation. Renaming someone in Scripture is always significant and means much more than a shift in social media handle. Renaming holds value in describing expectations for a future relationship with God. People grow into their names over time, like a promise of who you are becoming. The question "What's your name?" might best be translated as "What kind of person are you?" or "What are your values?" or "Who are you becoming?" in today's context.

A few chapters before the wrestling match, when Jacob's dad, Isaac, is dishing out blessings, Jacob is asked his name. He lies and claims to be his older brother, Esau. He knows *that* name is his ticket to the gravy train, so he pinches it without hesitation. This time around, when prompted to say who he is, Jacob tells the truth: his own name. This is a confession of sorts. He's admitting who he's been—a conniving, scheming trickster—revealed in the meaning of his name, Jacob. We're told his name derives from grabbing his womb mate, Esau, by the heel when they are born. It marks him as slimy and deceitful. Calling himself Jacob is akin to admitting he's a cheat.

Before this, Jacob has always wanted *things*: Esau's birthright, Isaac's inheritance, and Laban's sheep; but now he wants an *identity*. A name. Something other than his label as a charlatan, crook, and shark. He wants to acknowledge who he really is, not just who he's been pretending to be. Perhaps he's in the process of becoming Israel—one who wrestles with God—but still retains some Jacob tendencies. Most of us have been there more times than we care to admit. We desperately want to be more like Jesus, but the moment someone cuts us off on the freeway, we dissolve into the pettiest version of ourselves. (Just me?) Like Jacob, we are still in the process of becoming who we are meant to be. We are still in the process of making our lives declare what we say we believe. Even Jacob's new name narrates an ongoing process, one that is never complete. To be "one who contends with God" suggests action, tension, and future wrestling, not arrival or completion.

The other major thing that shifts here is Jacob's hip. Literally. This is not a mark of weakness or punishment in the passage. The new name and new limp are signs of his blessing and covenant with God. The limp is a badge of Jacob's strength and unrelenting determination, a reminder that he fought, persevered, and would not let go, all night long. Lionel Richie would be proud. The limp is a sign of the prophetic witness that God invites wrestling to create transformation. God even initiates the fight! To consider the limp as a punishment completely misses the way it is described in the passage. It is likely some arrive at that understanding through internalized narratives of disability as punitive. Wrestling reveals something about Jacob we haven't observed up until this point in the story: He's a fighter. He's tenacious. He's a survivor. Maybe he sings Destiny's Child to psych himself up too. He'll hang on, clinging to the angel until he's blessed. This struggle becomes his new identity: one who strives with God, instead of trying to outpace God.

If we backtrack a little bit in Genesis 32, we recognize that this is the first time Jacob asks God to save him. He prays for deliverance right before the angel appears. Jacob is scared his brother will make good on the promise to kill him. He cries out to the God of his father to rescue him from the consequences of his swindling lifestyle. This is what God's deliverance looks like: wrestling, all night long, to transform Jacob into Israel. Something tells me that a physical wrestling match with an angel isn't exactly what Jacob had in mind when he prayed for liberation. "God, please dislocate my hip" isn't likely to be found next to a HE>i bumper sticker any time soon. Yet this is how God brings restorative healing to Jacob, whether we can market it or not.

The divine encounter doesn't just change Jacob's name and physicality; it heals Jacob, transforming his perspective. Before this, he's ready to wheel and deal everyone out of reputation, inheritance, and sheep. Who cares that he has cheated his brother, lied to his dad, and tricked his uncle? That is the price to pay for the cushy lifestyle full of health and wealth that he named and claimed. He's manufacturing his own prosperity through materialistic gain. The chapter even lists the number of goats (220), camels (30), and cows (40) that Jacob owns. He's got it made! By every external marker, he's living his best life. He left

Canaan with nothing and returns with a serious entourage that is Instagram-ready: two camps full of stuff and servants. Jacob believes he got it all by relying on his own hard work and conniving schemes. He doesn't think he needs God or God's provision, which reveals the fable of independence common among nondisabled people, even today. He's living the myth of scarcity that so many of us have inherited: that we must continue the rat race of workaholism to manufacture our own success.

Pre-wrestling match, Jacob's faith is one of fickle allegiance in which he retains his own insurance policy in case God doesn't pay out. "Sure, God will bless me," Jacob muses, "but I'll need to wear goatskin and defraud my dad to get the lifestyle I want." Jacob doesn't fully understand who God is or how blessings function until he is disabled. Predictably, all the stuff he accumulates doesn't satisfy Jacob or mend his relationship with his twin brother. He constantly yearns for more. He can't stop at one spouse, a couple of sons, and a humble herd of livestock. He continues to take, take, take more stuff to fill the void of his insecurity. He wants to hustle his way to outearning and outpacing the need to rely on God. He believes his net worth has made him worthy. He finally acknowledges who he really is—a schemer—and calls out to the God of his dad to deliver him from this vicious cycle of radical independence. He finally stops trying to fix everything and learns dependence on the living God.

"Deliver me!" he pleads. Enter angel, ready to wrestle. Let's Get Ready to Rumble!

It's easy for us to think this is a bit harsh. Should the angel *fight* Jacob? What's this angel's problem? Does Jacob's hip need to be wrenched out? These are valid and important questions for us to wrestle with. (See what I did there?) Yet, when we focus too much on the answers to these questions, we miss what the passage zooms in on. The fight produces a healing transformation for Jacob. God's provision isn't more stuff or even physical fitness; it's God's presence showing up, willing to grapple with Jacob in his despair. The wrestling match disables Jacob and produces the first sign of his transformative healing in the narrative: a dislocated hip. In the next chapter, Jacob is repentant, weeping, and generous, offering Esau all the property that was once so precious. You know, the goods Jacob conned his family into forking over. He's finally stopped swindling and started serving. Humbled, Jacob calls himself Esau's servant, and entreats, "Accept my present from my hand. For I have seen your face, which is like seeing the face of God, and you have accepted me. Please accept my blessing that is brought to you, because God has dealt graciously with me, and because I have enough" (Gen. 33:10–11 ESV).

Converted from the duplicitous conspirator we've known up to this point, Jacob declares that Esau is an image-bearer, one who reflects God to him. This disabling encounter heals Jacob from his competition with his brother and brings an end to the sibling rivalry that previously controlled him. Instead of stealing blessings, he's dishing them out. Instead of hoarding material possessions, he's giving them away. He finally trusts that he doesn't need to do it all on his own, and even describes his disabling combat with God's delegate as "gracious." We get the sense that Jacob is changing into the Israel he's meant to become: a forgiving, humble, generous person who witnesses God in those he used to despise. An Israel with a limp.

It is imperative that we interpret the limp as a gracious blessing, as Jacob does. He doesn't have to keep striving and swindling, earning his blessings through cashmere cosplay. He can take off the costume and show everyone his struggle with God by limping along and leaning on his walking stick. There's no hiding who he is anymore. Instead, this story is about the ways God shows up, willing to wrestle and transform Jacob into a generous and humble version of himself. Liberated from manufacturing malicious schemes, Jacob learns to trust God. Faith, then, looks like wrestling—all night long—and emerging with a healing limp.

Describing Jacob in the cloud of witnesses, Hebrews 11 tells us, "Later, when Jacob was about to die, he leaned on his walking stick and worshiped. Then because of his faith he blessed each of Joseph's sons" (v. 21 CEV). Jacob's picture of faithfulness includes worshiping, cane in hand, and blessing the next generation. I treasure this image, because it allows me to envision my limp as part of my healing instead of something that must be cured or killed off in hopes of inspiring nondisabled people. I picture a gentle Yoda figure propped up by his cane as he imparts wisdom to the next generation. "Judge me by my size, do you?" Jacob's faith feels like leaning on a cane, unable to meet the world's definition of a hustler but making it into the hall of faith simply for worshiping and blessing others. His limp becomes a beautiful reminder of this transformative encounter. Instead of curing Jacob or killing him off, Scripture introduces a disability that tethers him to the graciousness of the living God.

There is a lot that limping has taught me over the years. Using my cane and wheelchair has given me a different perspective on who I am and who God is. There's a freedom in using mobility devices that's tricky for nondisabled people to understand. It's a relief to have something carry my body to spaces not accessible to me on foot. Wheelchairs mean freedom, many disability activists proclaim, because they allow us to move about the world with greater ease and agency. We don't consider our wheels confining because they aid our mobility and individuality. I am quicker and more agile in my chair than on my legs. Using my wheelchair is far less painful, too. But it's also liberating when I use my cane or wheelchair because everyone knows about my disability. It becomes visible and palatable to people. It's a window into the parts of my everyday life that are sometimes invisible to people who do not know my story.

There's a freedom in using mobility devices that acknowledges the limits of my body and declares that I can't do it all by myself, and that's not something to be ashamed of. In fact, for an Enneagram 1, recovering know-it-all, that's liberating for me. None of us do it alone. All of us are dependent on one another for survival. It's simply that we've collectively decided which aspects of interdependence are more socially acceptable than others. Almost everyone I know drinks coffee, yet few people I know grow and grind their own coffee beans. Everyone I know wears clothes, but no one I know sews an entire wardrobe. Folks routinely wear glasses or contacts without knowing how to manufacture them and without the threat of prayerful perpetrators trying to cure them. Many people I know use an iPhone (or even an Android, because I, too, am a friend of sinners), yet no one I know created the tech behind smartphones. These examples are based on my cultural context, but the point remains: we are all part of an interdependent web of connectivity, whether we care to admit it or not. It's just that some forms of interdependence are considered normative and others are considered tragic. Those of us who are disabled already know how to welcome interdependence as a habitual practice without demonizing our bodies in the process.

We, the disabled, know what it means to live in a way that is dependent on something other than ourselves for survival, and we realize that all the world's systems—capitalism, health care, the economy—are not established with us or for us. "Nothing about us, without us," is our disability rights slogan, because so many systems have left us out. We do not benefit from these dominions of darkness in the way that most nondisabled people do, and therefore the systems reject us. But the truth is that we are liberated from the bondage to independence and workaholism that does not promote anyone's flourishing. We don't have to prove our worth or outearn everyone around us. (Looking at you, Jacob.) We live on the other side of the myth of independence. We are threatening to the system because we render it obsolete and meaningless. We are the face of difference. We declare with our bodies that the system is a fickle farce in which we refuse to participate. We don't rely on our bodies to praise God, but have a deeper sense of who God is because of our acknowledged interdependence.

Even our pain is a prayer. Death and disease do not scare us because we live close to the edge of them. We have looked death in the eye and declared that it has no victory over us. We declare the truth that we are from ash and will return to ash one day, and that day might be sooner than we plan. But our bodies proclaim what the Creator can do with a bit of ash. My body refuses the cultural script handed to it by an ableist society, and for that, I am so grateful for my disability. I just wish my body hadn't been tortured for so long to learn this truth.

God's desire is for transformative relationship, not productivity or independence. God doesn't want Jacob to manufacture prosperity or swear an empty oath of allegiance to an insurance-policy faith. Instead, God is willing to wrestle for Jacob to learn how to limp. God is after transformation and healing, even when it manifests differently than we expect. In recounting this combat, Hosea tells us that Jacob is weeping during the encounter with the angel (Hosea 12:2–5). This reminds me of Jesus, sweating drops of blood, begging for the cup to be removed, pleading to not have to go through with the pain of the cross. Jesus is in anguish. Just as in Jacob's story, an angel appears to strengthen Jesus. Just like Jacob, Jesus's body bears the disabling marks of redemption.[15]

---

15. Check out Martin Albl, "'For Whenever I Am Weak, Then I Am Strong': Disability in Paul's Epistles," in *This Able Body*, ed. Hector Avalos, Sarah J. Melcher, and Jeremy Schipper (Atlanta: Society of Biblical Literature, 2007), 149.

In its first incarnation, Israel is disabled, physically marked by Jacob's wild encounter with God. Later generations figuratively participate in the disability covenant by not eating the sinew of the thigh muscle when consuming meat. This isn't one of the laws prescribed to them: it's something they choose to do to partake in this covenant-making moment with their disabled leader. Every time they butchered an animal, they were reminded of Jacob's disability through this embodied practice. We do the same today by partaking of the Lord's Table. In eating the bread and drinking from the cup, we remember Jesus's disabled body. We participate in the cross by taking the elements together and deepening our trust in God's graciousness, even in the midst of our wrestling. The table is where we can forget about hording stuff for ourselves and recognize that there is enough for *all* of us. The table is where we realize God isn't embarrassed by who we have been, even with our Jacob tendencies. The table is where we can limp with God to redemption.

Both the covenant and the cross are marked by disability. Jacob reminds us that this is how disability functions in Scripture: as part of a blessing from God on the road to redemption. This is the story of disability that the church needs to start telling: the one where disability is a blessing that future generations choose to participate in, because it acts as a redemptive sign of the covenant with a gracious God. We need a new language of embodiment and healing that is not coated in the residue of ableism. We need to tell new stories about disability that allow us to exist in all our complexity without categorizing us as suffering or sinning. We need to start telling the story that disability can be a blessing from God. Maybe then we can know what it means to be healed.

REFLECTION AND RESPONSE

▶ Consider what you watch. Find examples of movies, pop culture, and TV shows where disability is not villainized or reduced to a metaphor. You might start with *Crip Camp: A Disability Revolution* (2020) or *The Peanut Butter Falcon* (2019). Host a watch party and discuss the film with your friends.

▶ Recover disability narratives in Scripture. Are you surprised to find disability considered as a blessing or a mark of the covenant for Jacob? How can disability be celebrated when you partake of the Lord's Table? How can you recover disability as part of this narrative to celebrate the prophetic witness of disabled people in your community?

▶ Create a piece of (visual, musical, poetic, movement) art in any medium and style celebrating Jacob's disability as a blessing and a mark of the covenant, as discussed in this chapter. How might this art inspire change in your own community? Consider hosting a (digital) art exhibit to showcase everyone's responses to Jacob's disability as a blessing.

TOP TEN
"I Know How You Feels"

Folks say these to me when they are trying to empathize with being disabled.

10. My friend/cousin/coworker/barista is disabled . . . so I know how you feel.

9. I burned myself out after partying all weekend . . . so I know how you feel.

8. I sprained my ankle back in third grade . . . so I know how you feel.

7. I get exhausted when I walk all day too.

6. One time I had an ingrown toenail removed, so I know how you feel about doctors.

5. I had to go to physical therapy for six whole weeks after I busted my knee.

4. I was wheeled out after giving birth, so I know how hard wheelchairs can be to use.

3. Aren't we all just a little bit disabled?

2. We all have something. That's just your cross to bear. My boss is mean.

1. I think I have a little bit of what you have.

Disability Mosquitos

Y ou're too sensitive," he insists, like he's trying to swat away a fly. We are rehashing a conversation where one too many disability metaphors was used. We each recall the exchange with a similar fiery color palate, but in different hues. His recollection is all spontaneous explosion. He recalls that I immediately detonated when he used one little word that *is* in the dictionary, by the way. He checked and informed me it's the second definition, so it's permissible for him to use. He was dejected by how humiliated I made him feel by telling him not to use disability as a metaphor. Evidently, it's not just that I'm too sensitive about disability, but that I'm polluting others with that sensitivity too. He's distraught because this is too much to keep up with while preaching. "Besides," he adds, "the gospel is *meant* to offend."

My memory of the incident is slightly less spontaneous explosion and more of a pressure-building, erupting volcano. During a discussion about Zacchaeus's healing, I am preoccupied with deciding how to handle the disability-as-metaphor elephant in the room. I am lost in the metaphor maze, no longer present in the contours of the discussion about a tax collector climbing a sycamore tree and giving half his money to the poor. It's like how the adults speak in Charlie Brown's world: all "Wah Wah" and no substance. "Wah Wah *crippling* Wah Wah Wah *paralyzing* Wah Wah *blinding* Wah Wah."

The first spark, I let go. Disability isn't a metaphor for weakness, but I don't want to be the language police. The second burst, my jaw tenses, but I brush off the upsurge. I don't want to launch into a whole thing on disability language when I want to discuss how Zacchaeus's example encourages ecclesiastical reparation for our community. I want to talk about how his healing doesn't include any physical change or curing but alters his social station, revitalizing his life to one of coflourishing by giving his possessions away.[1] I want to talk about how healing is not about the physical form but about transformation for this little person. So I steady myself to remain focused, to remain dormant. The third spur, I consider saying something but decide against it, digging my fingernails into my palm, the pressure of my emotions and cuticles mounting. By the fourth time disability is used as a metaphor for weakness in less than ten minutes, I interject with impatience. Curtly, I erupt, "Can we stop using *blind* as a metaphor?"

The words are barely out of my mouth before he rejoinders with, "Well, it's in the Bible."

Thus begin several hours of clean-up conversation, all about how I'm too sensitive and, what's worse, making him feel dejected. He felt attacked that I called him out. I should know him better than to think he's ableist. I don't want to hurt anyone's feelings or fight over language, but this is bigger than a he-said, she-said jumble of emotions. It's not solely about language, either. The problem with centering his emotions is that doing so means refusing to take responsibility for how words scorch

---

1. Bethany McKinney Fox, *Disability and the Way of Jesus: Holistic Healing in the Gospels and the Church* (Downers Grove, IL: IVP Academic, 2019), 144–45.

marginalized groups and instead uses the dictionary and the Bible to justify the burn. Blindness isn't in the Zacchaeus narrative. It was superimposed on the text without much consideration for whom it was harming. And while it's true that blindness is sometimes metaphorical in Scripture, that doesn't automatically give us a free pass to use the metaphor without care.

Murder. Slavery. Rape. Genocide. Very specific rules about menstruation, circumcision, and diets are in the Holy Book too. There's even a talking donkey. I've never heard any preacher claim we need to listen to donkeys hee-haw to remain "biblical." Or that women should drill a tent peg into a house guest's skull, but that's in there too. Just ask Jael. The fact that something is in the Bible doesn't mean the Bible is instructing us to do it. I am certainly not the first one to point out that Scripture features all kinds of head-scratching, stomach-churning wacky tales that we don't take as prescriptive for everyday, modern life. Most of us know there is a difference between prescription (what the Bible tells us to *do*) and description (what the Bible tells us *about*). To blame the Bible for using disability as a metaphor for weakness is missing the point. Nowhere in the Bible does it command, "Thou shalt use ableist metaphors."

But Jesus uses disability as a metaphor, so that makes it okay, right? News flash: we are not Jesus. If we want to make an argument that we follow whatever Jesus did exactly, we must get real with ourselves. Jesus undresses to wash the disciples' feet at Passover (John 13:4), which I have never seen reenacted in a church setting despite attending many a church play. Jesus braids a whip to drive people out of the temple for selling cattle, sheep, and doves (John 2:15). I've been to many a church marketplace (read: bookshop, coffeehouse, or a hybrid complete with G>∧∨ water bottle stickers) but have never heard of one shut down via whip. Jesus likely didn't wear deodorant, use toilet paper, or drive a car, and most churchy people I know do all those things without any theological conundrums.

You might think these are all somewhat silly examples, but they reveal a deeper inconsistency when we claim to follow every single thing that Jesus does. It doesn't bear out in our lives, not because of sin or hypocrisy, but because we recognize that we are equipped with the Spirit to discern what is cultural or temporal and what is universal. Strictly adhering to everything Jesus does as prescriptive undermines the role of the Holy Spirit. Do we really trust the Spirit if we must follow Jesus like robots, without discerning context? Do we really believe Scripture is living and active if we legalistically apply its language and letters as stagnant? If we read Scripture in and with community, we should be willing to learn from the gifts of that community and move beyond thinking about Scripture simply as a self-help book or how-to guide. It is so much more than Basic Instructions Before Leaving Earth. Scripture is not YouTube.

Then my own relationship to biblical interpretation was disparaged. I was grilled, asked whether I was more loyal to the sacredness of Scripture or to my disability community. I have been called the language police, social justice warrior, PC patrol, and a snowflake who just needs to take a chill pill. I wouldn't mind a chill pill, but my insurance probably wouldn't cover it. I am still filing claims for my *actual* medications.

These retorts suggest I am the problem for pointing out the assumptions behind someone's language instead of the language causing harm on its own. They represent a refusal to take responsibility for the ways that words burn people and a desire to remain above the heat, relying on the dictionary and the Bible to justify using expired words and metaphors. This doesn't smell like Jesus (2 Cor. 2:15). Did it occur to this pastor that I am not calling him out, but calling him *in* to a more inclusive way, one that centers the least of these like Jesus? Did he consider that my engagement with his words isn't an act of cancellation or condemnation, but one of conviction? Did he stop to consider that perhaps I am not oversensitive, but he is under-aware of perspectives other than his own? Did he wonder whether I might not be the only one harmed by casually using disability as a metaphor?

Metaphors rely on a shared understanding of an experience to convey meaning. They take something unknown, connect it to something known, and create an emotional attachment in the process. They are the way we express feelings or describe big, complicated concepts. We use metaphor to explain ourselves. I am tempted to use one right here, but I will save you the meta eye roll. The problem is when this emotional and experiential attachment is created on my back. Or, more accurately, on my lame leg. To use my body as a symbol, to equate my body to something embarrassing or undesirable, produces an emotional link at the expense of my experience. Using disability as a metaphor "others" disabled people. Blind, deaf, mute, lame, crippled, dumb are all frequent metaphors predicated on the idea that the bodies and minds of one-quarter of the US population are unwelcome or unworthy. If you think using these metaphors isn't so bad, ask yourself this: Have you ever heard them used in a positive way? Has "lame" ever meant anything good? Have you ever experienced "crippled" as something powerful? Disability metaphors allow everyone to agree that my body is bad.

I am not your metaphor. My body is not your symbol to use. My crippled body and lame leg do not give you permission to dismiss me as symbolic for whatever you find difficult. Being told over and over again that your body is immoral is exhausting. No, that meeting was not "paralyzing" or "crippling" or "blinding," unless it was physically paralyzing, crippling, or blinding.

Language is a repository for our biases. It carries centuries of shameful ideologies about disability. When we choose a word to convey an idea, it's like facing a vending machine; we must select from what is already there. (If the vending machine had thousands of adjectives, that is.) When we face a vending machine, parched and in need of liquid comfort, we summon the chocolate milk—desiring it to wrap us in its silky sheets. We know exactly what to expect, and it won't disappoint. Our desperation is like a "Got Milk?" commercial with the metallic clank of the vending machine as its soundtrack. Hello chocolate milk, old friend.

But sometimes the food in the vending machine is expired. We didn't realize it when we pressed E6, but once the expiration date stares us down, we wouldn't glug chunky milk. We might consider it, briefly, with all the rationalization of an angsty adolescent: "No one can tell *me* what to drink!" But eventually, its sour fumes would convince us otherwise. Stomach in somersaults, we come to our senses and put down the bottle. Congealed cow is not worth the trip to the commode. Nothing can persuade us we are not thirsty faster than fumes emanating from rancid milk.

We should act at least as conscientiously with language about disabled people as we do with vending machines.

We might have assumed it was acceptable to use a certain word or metaphor; and perhaps at one point it was unobjectionable in our social circles. But once we recognize that the word is expired, we should put down the putrid chocolate milk and drink something else. There are other drinks to be gulped. Grabbing what is right in front of you, even when it is past the expiration date, causes internal damage, discomfort, and expulsion, whether it is intended or not. Disability slurs are past the expiration date. Using disability as a metaphor is past the expiration date. Resisting change that will benefit the least of these is past the expiration date.

Language is constantly evolving. None of us use the perfect word all the time. But all of us can respond with grace and compassion when we are confronted with our own embedded assumptions. This isn't about following the latest social justice trend. It's about loving our neighbors enough to use words that don't harm them. It's about getting honest with our own assumptions when it comes to the hierarchy of image-bearers that we have manufactured without realizing it. It's about being able to interpret my disabled body as holy and redeemed, like the body of our resurrected, disabled Christ.

"That's not how I meant it," he counters. "It doesn't mean that anymore," they snap. I want to commiserate with folks who don't mean the harm they cause. I can attest that they are often genuine. They honestly didn't know that was a wounding thing to say. Grace to you, friend. We have all been there: said the wrong thing, used the wrong phrase, not realized the damage of our well-intentioned words. Life is a language lesson. I empathize with good intentions. But there is a big difference between intent and impact. It is easy to diminish the impact of your actions by focusing on the intent behind them. You didn't *mean* to be ableist, so you can't be ableist, or something like that. That seems polite, and maybe you can assure yourself of that idea for a time, but it doesn't hold up in real life.

When you accidentally bump into someone at the grocery store, you say "sorry" and make sure the person is unharmed. You didn't mean to hit them. Perhaps *they* were too absorbed in their text messages to notice they were traipsing across the aisle, but you still check that they are not hurt by the chance collision. No polite, reasonable person would suggest you willfully crashed into someone else if you apologize. In fact, no one even mentions intent, because it's largely irrelevant to the situation. Same thing happens when you accidentally give your friends food poisoning when cooking them dinner. No one stops to declare it was not premeditated. Honestly, how suspicious would that be? If you are in a friendship context where people assume that you devised some elaborate pasta plot to poison a friend, you might want to get new friends. No one cares whether you *meant* to poison your friends. They are still bent over the toilet, tasting your carbonara in reverse. So you apologize. Profusely.

Maybe even with a silly pasta pun, like "sorry for the im-pasta" or "I'm tortellini sorry" to make them chuckle.

Focusing solely on your emotions suggests that your intent is the only metric when it comes to harm. Not everything is about you. It also pretends that we cause damage only when we intend to, which anyone who has ever had food poisoning knows is untrue. Regardless of whether you intend to harm disabled people, slurs hurt us. Words cut us down. Metaphors using our bodies as undesirable shame us. Sticking to using "lame" or "blind" instead of being willing to change damages us.

Everyone wants to believe they are the exception to the rule, that somehow they have grown up in an ableist world but never internalized ableist language, tendencies, or ideas. This is not true, even for disabled people. Ableism is the air we all breathe. Like most idols, the idea that nondisabled bodies are perfect and good makes itself invisible, so we don't notice we're worshiping them. We are fooled into thinking disability is corrupt, ugly, and unwanted, so we never second-guess this. All the while, we are worshiping the world's notion of perfection instead of the vehement goodness between us that God adores.

Whenever I invite someone to rethink their language, I am taking the time to invest in them instead of dismissing them as a lost cause. Accountability is an invitation to address the ways we've internalized the dominions of darkness and crucify them. Any time I tell someone their vending machine choice is ableist, I am hoping against hope that they are willing to crucify the dominions of darkness that hold them captive. More often than not, they are unwilling. They would rather live in a world that poisons me than one where we can all flourish freely.

As people who claim to love our neighbors, we can aspire to more than simply "not harming" people—we can become proactive in listening to the pain we cause. It will feel bumpy at times, but we are not called to be comfortable: we are called to love one another. We can move beyond our fears and love our neighbors enough to stretch ourselves. Fear tells us that we must feel shame when we get it wrong, but love is elastic enough to embrace the whole self—disability accommodations, expired vending machine words, and all. Love is the model given to first-century churches grappling with fractured viewpoints on how to live the Jesus way.

When hostility threatened to divide first-century churches, John proclaimed, "There is no fear in love, but perfect love casts out fear; for fear has to do with punishment, and whoever fears has not reached perfection in love" (1 John 4:18). I wish people loved me enough to cast out their fear of being wrong. I wish people loved me enough to stretch their understanding of embodiment and disability language. I wish people loved me enough to crucify the dominions of darkness they've internalized. I wish people loved me enough to change.

There will be times when we don't fully understand someone else's pain or when we wonder if the person is too easily triggered. Who cares? Loving our neighbors shouldn't be reserved for times we agree with or understand or feel comfortable with them. In fact, we don't really need to try to love people who are just like us. That's uniformity, not unity. We should love our neighbors enough to take their emotions seriously. We should love them enough to say sorry when we inadvertently food poison them. We should love them enough to believe them.

When Paul is writing to a divided church, he instructs them to "share each other's burdens, and in this way obey the law of Christ" (Gal. 6:2 NLT). He teaches them to consider other people's wounds as their own. For nondisabled Jesus followers, this should include considering the concerns of the disability community. We should care about the pain of our neighbors, even when we don't fully understand it. Even when you think I'm oversensitive.

In doing this, we are fulfilling the law of Christ. It's not about having the "correct" theology or believing all the same things.

It's not some intellectual assent to lofty ideals. It's not even about being right. The law of Christ is fulfilled when we take another's burdens as seriously as we take our own. This is how we facilitate coflourishing. This is what neighbor love looks like in practice: Realizing that you might not understand my pain but committing to taking it seriously. Listening instead of gaslighting. Believing instead of doubting. Perhaps then, love can cast out our fears of getting it wrong and stretch us enough to be in community with one another.

Whenever I'm informed that I'm oversensitive for asking someone to stop using disability slurs or metaphors, I wonder what the barometer for sensitivity is. Is there an accepted rubric somewhere I don't know about? Casting me as oversensitive assumes that microaggressions are overblown. Microaggressions are like mosquito bites. When you rarely get bitten, they aren't a big deal. Sure, your skin is itchy and a little puffy, but after a day of intermittent scratching, you erase the incident from your memory with ease. Mosquito, who? Microaggressions are dismissed as minuscule, like mosquito bites, because they seem fleeting.

But when you are bitten dozens of times in a day, mosquito bites are less of a pest and more of a pestilence. Goose bumps spread across your body: persistent prickly tingles on your every hair follicle. You are no longer able to hear anything except the pulsing nettles nagging your raw skin. "Scratch me," the bites beckon—louder, shriller, rowdier, until it's all you can hear.

When your body is littered with mosquito bites, your awareness of their puffy, itchy presence is intensified. Mosquitos might be mini, but their impact, especially en masse, can be monumental. The mosquito is the most dangerous animal on the planet, killing more humans every year than any other animal.[2] To brush them off as pests simply because they are pesky is ignorant. It focuses on their minuscule size instead of their mammoth impact.

My skin is a mosquito minefield.

- "You're such an inspiration," a classmate applauds me. "I would kill myself if I had what you have." Bite.
- Someone at my church "names and claims" that if I just had enough faith, I could rise out of my wheelchair. Bite.
- A stranger cusses me out in the Target parking lot, yelling that I'm not *really* disabled. I'm just faking it for pity. Bite.
- Channel surfing in the car on the way to work one Monday, the radio blares, "There's a lot of lame guys out there." Bite.
- "You should be so grateful for your husband," a friend enlightens me. "Not everyone would *put up with* your disability." Bite.
- A colleague uses "lame" as a slur while we wait for our iced mochas. "Hey, not cool. *I* am lame," I muster. They reply: "Oh, I wasn't talking about *you*. I don't even think of you as disabled." Bite.

Each of these is a trifling bite, imperceptible to everyone around me, but eventually, I am covered in mosquito mounds from head to toe, ableism malaria pounding beneath my enflamed, raw skin.

Even now, some will wonder, but what's the big deal? It's *just* a mosquito bite. It's not their fault that *you* already have so many mosquito bites. True. But why would you want to keep infecting

2. Daniel Jameson, "The 10 Most Dangerous Animals in the World," *Condé Nast Traveller*, May 1, 2019, https://www.cntraveller.com/gallery/the-10-most-dangerous -animals-in-the-world. This article lists mosquitos as the most dangerous animal on the planet, after humans.

someone if you had the chance to prevent it? We bring insect repellent with us to the woods. We take preventative antimalarials when traveling. We post warning signs at the park if there's even a chance of West Nile virus. We buy mosquito nets. Why wouldn't we do the same with ableism?

It's not about avoiding a list of words. It's about rethinking what those words mean, what they assume, and how they impact people around you. Disability as a metaphor and disability slurs are widely used without people so much as noticing. But *I* notice. It is harmful not just to me or even to an entire community of disabled humans; it is destructive to all of us, whether we realize it or not. No wonder people interpret my body as damaged when our language portrays it as such. No wonder people pity me and think I am worth less when I can't walk, when our language constantly confirms this idea to us. Our words are the vehicle for ranking our bodies within an artificial hierarchy, one that claims disability is cruel, subhuman, and bears less of God's image.

It's not just a word, but all the assumptions underneath the word. Using "lame" as a slur or "blind" as a metaphor might not seem like a big deal to you. But when you are regularly dismissed as bad, wrong, ugly, and worth exterminating, it is another voice telling you that your body is the worst-case scenario. My life is worth living. My body is a holy temple. My lame leg displays the image of God to the world. I should not be the butt of your jokes or the tragedy of your nightmares. I am not your metaphor.

It is easy to write a story with a villain. We can even share a fickle intimacy over hating the same people for a minute. It fuels many an angry Twitter rant and explosive Facebook post. But the predicament we find ourselves in as Jesus followers is that we are to love our enemies because they are not our true adversary. There are no good and evil people, just harmful actions done by people who bear God's image. The people who become our enemies have a face, have a name, have a story. They make me dinner when I can't walk. They lift my scooter into my car. The folks who do ableist things are the same people that I call my friends and family.

The pastor who begins this chapter is one who loves our community well. One who proactively reserved a close parking space for me so I could attend an event. One who is not my enemy. Like most folks I know, this pastor did not *intend* to be ableist. But all that ableism requires of you is to leave accepted language and practices alone. Don't touch anything. Just leave everything the way it already is. You don't have to harbor ableist intentions for ableism to injure (disabled) people. That's how dominions of darkness work. They are so seeped into our practices and ideas that we barely notice they are there. We fool ourselves into thinking that's just the way it is, without realizing we *made* it that way.

When we claim disability is part of a social construct, we forget that we are its construction workers. We hammer in its words, metaphors, movies, pop culture, books, and op-eds. We chisel out a hierarchy of humanity based on its ideas. When the prevailing images, stories, and concepts about disabled people are limiting and negative, you come to believe that those ideas are true. This is an immersive process that typically happens without awareness or consent. We are segregated from disabled people and fed a diet of inspiration porn and burden ballads about a whole community of human beings. It is not simply malicious, spiteful trolls who are ableist. It is your pastor who loves the community. It is your beloved coach who cares for students. It is your colleague who volunteers at the old folks' home. It is your Sunday school teacher who taught you "Jesus loves me." It is your friend whom you cherish. And it might even be you.

The good news is the story doesn't end there. Jesus defeated the dominions of darkness, so we don't have to live in them. You can help shift the ongoing power of ableism by doing the internal work of changing your language. You can welcome us by making sure we are celebrated for who we are instead of shamed for what we cannot do. You can build more accessible spaces by learning when your vending machine choice accidentally poisoned us. You can make space for disabled people to lead inside the beloved community. You can become DEET.

My shivering arms rattle my surgical bracelets against the crispy paper on the exam table. Everything around me is pale: the walls, the medical cabinets, the fluorescent lighting; it's as if they interpreted "sterile environment" as removing all color and warmth from the world. The radiologist whose every sentence ends with "bro" sets up the CT scan while I lie facedown on the table and they brand me with *Xs* for the injection sites. Their blue scrubs are the only color in the room.

I am a mark, a target, an *X* without a face or a name. My every identity marker has been removed or concealed so the surgeons can focus on the problem that is my disabled body. I wonder to myself whether they ever treat the wrong leg, with how much Sharpie I am now wearing. I wonder how long it will take for the stain of their impatience to rub off.

"Make sure to remain perfectly still so the surgeon doesn't paralyze you," a nurse instructs me. They tell me not to make any jokes, not to ask questions, not to disrupt them while they work. I must lie awake, yet stationary; conscious, yet silent; alert, yet relaxed, so they can track the surgical equipment inside my body. I am a zombie, but not one anyone buys a ticket to see.

My main concern during the procedure is, what if I need to fart? Do I hold it? Push it out and risk jolting the surgical equipment? Can they somehow see gas on the CT scan? Suddenly it dawns on me that there were no flatulence facts in the library of medical literature they forced down my throat before the procedure. I open my lips to ask, but I've already been censured for making a joke with bro-surgeon, so I hold in my words and my farts until further notice.

"Do you have someone to drive you home?" the blue scrubs ask, one too many times. They are not even done stabbing me before they are ready to ditch me there on the frigid table. I count the number of times one of them tells me I am brave or strong. I hit double digits before the big hand on the clock switches numbers.

Every person who passes by my recovery room gapes at me like I am a child trying to buy a toy with my own allowance for the first time. I am the circus freak, the pain exhibit, the corpse reanimated after death, ready for a parade of voyeuristic whispers and condescending side-eyes. "She's a tough cookie," I hear one of them whisper. "She was brave in there," a nurse convinces her colleague.

Brave. Strong. Courageous. Fighter. Survivor. All words used to describe me that afternoon. The identity envelopes me the more that people insist it is true. Like the red allergy bracelet around my wrist screaming "codeine" to the distracted doctors. They might as well give me a bracelet that brands me "brave"!

I don't want to be brave. I just want to be human. I am drained, swollen, and stiff. I am not sure I have it in me to be strong too. I know it is well-meaning, but the more that people insist I am brave, the more they cast me as a superhuman who is not in need of support and tender care. When I said I wanted to be Wonder Woman, it was so people didn't think I was a burden, not so people didn't care for my burdens. It feels more like a condemnation than a compliment: a spiritual bypassing of sorts, where they don't have to get involved in my liberation from ableism because I am strong enough to endure the pain of it. I *am* a fighter, but what if I don't have to be?

How can I be human when I am just an *X* in a sterile, pale room? How can I share my feelings when people are too quick to dismiss them as oversensitive? How can I acknowledge my pain when people only want to praise my bravery? How can these attitudes not have transformed in the two decades that I have been disabled?

There's a liberty that comes with life-as-you-know-it ending when you are eleven. It gives you freedom to take risks, to mess up, to live with verve. After all, what's going to happen? Are you going to end up in a wheelchair? Been there, done that, got the T-shirt. Really. One of my physical therapists gave me a "no pain, no gain" T-shirt without any sense of irony. I have already endured what most people think is the worst-case scenario: becoming disabled. And yet, most days, I am still kicking.

I think about all my body has taught me, how I have learned to live outside of clocks and calendars. How I have learned to value myself, not as a résumé of accomplishments, but as someone with worth simply because I radiate God's image to an unsuspecting world.

I think about how I have survived, over and over and over again through medical trauma and housing discrimination, through academic advocacy and supermarket lawsuits, through people dismissing my pain. I think about how I am willing to take on Goliaths (hello, medical-industrial complex) because they do not scare me. They have already subjected me to their engulfing procedures and burning tests, but I am fireproof. I am a new creation, one that has been forged by fire, affliction, and courage.

But some days, I would still like to go out into the world without my fireproof armor, without anticipating that a swarm of ableist mosquitos awaits me on the other side. I would like to live in a world where my bravery is not the price of admission. Where I get to be myself: full of moxie and mess ups, sarcasm and snarky quips, never taking myself too seriously. I would like to live in a world where knowing silence is expected over the fickle comfort of platitudes, where strength isn't determined by how much pain you can endure before you break, where gaslighting isn't the expected response when I alert someone that their vending machine choice is expired, where compassion and justice are more important than the bravery that only develops in their absence.

I would like to be a full human and not just a metaphor. I would like to be me.

<hr>

REFLECTION AND RESPONSE

▶ Consider where you might have caused a mosquito bite for a disabled person without realizing it. Commit to eliminating two or three ableist phrases from your vocabulary each week. A useful list can be found at http://web.augsburg.edu /english/writinglab/Avoiding_Ableist_Language.pdf.

▶ Invite others to do the same. This is not about being the language police, or shaming people for using an expired vending machine choice. This is about shifting our perspective on disability so that we are not conflating it with something negative. One way to eliminate the shame of mosquito bites is to come up with fun alternatives to ableist words. Instead of "lame," try "cheesy" or "tacky" or even the *Gatsby* classic, "old hat."

▶ Do your homework. Learn from people writing about disability and faith with an open spirit. Here are some great places to start. Also check out the reading list in the back of this book.

  ▪ Shannon Dingle, "Resisting Ableism in the American Church," *Sojourners*, November 7, 2018, https://sojo .net/articles/resisting-ableism-american-church.

  ▪ Bethany McKinney Fox, *Disability and the Way of Jesus: Holistic Healing in the Gospels and the Church* (Downers Grove, IL: IVP Academic, 2019).

- Lamar Hardwick, *Disability and the Church: A Vision for Diversity and Inclusion* (Downers Grove, IL: Inter-Varsity, 2021).

- Lisa Sharon Harper, "Disability and Its Intersections," 2020, *Freedom Road*, podcast, featuring Shannon Dingle, Lisa Anderson, and Amy Kenny, https://freedom road.us/2020/06/2231.

- Christina Edmondson and Ekemini Uwan, with Andraéa LaVant, "Disability in the Church," October 9, 2021, *Truth's Table*, podcast, season 5, https://www .truthstable.com/season-5.

- Lynn Swedberg, "Dos and Don'ts for the Disability Ally," DisAbility Ministries Committee of the United Methodist Church, https://umcdmc.org/wp-content /uploads/2020/06/ableism_ally.pdf.

- John Swinton, "The Theology of Disability," September 8, 2017, in *Jude 3*, podcast, https://jude3project.org /podcast/disability.

- Stephanie Tait, *The View from Rock Bottom* (Eugene, OR: Harvest House, 2019).

- Amos Yong, *The Bible, Disability, and the Church: A New Vision of the People of God* (Grand Rapids: Eerdmans, 2011).

TOP TEN
Mosquito Swatters

Folks respond with these after I call out disability mosquitos.

10. It's not my fault *you* took offense.

9. You need a thicker skin.

8. Cancel culture is too much these days.

7. Your tone hurt my feelings.

6. You need to take a chill pill.

5. What ever happened to freedom of speech?

4. Who are you, the language police?

3. You are too sensitive.

2. It doesn't mean that anymore.

1. That's not how *I* meant it.

Disability Lessons

When he suddenly recoils into silence, I know something is wrong.

Checking in with my head physical therapist on a crisp Tuesday, my mood had rivaled that of the mockingbirds chirruping outside. We have the sarcastic rapport of a buddy comedy (working title: *The Cripped Crusader*). I tease that I've paid for so many appointments that I've practically bought his BMW. When he asks me how my leg is, I quip that it's "getting on my nerves." (Hint: It's a neurological condition. You see what I did there.)

We're halfway through this typical comedy routine when silence descends across his face. Whenever he's not down to clown, I know something is up. "Your hip is out," he mutters, the curve of his lip barbed downward. "Out of . . . [*inhale . . . inhale . . .*] what?" I wonder aloud.

Yep, it was out of the socket. I thought my body was doing so well. All the physical markers were right. Hair on my leg—check. Muscle mass comparable to my right side—check. Wiggling toes—check. Temperature above 90 degrees—check. By every external marker, I was living my best disabled life. Uh-oh.

Turns out the mockingbirds weren't singing with me at all. They were mocking my glee.

The paper covering the examination table was now as crumpled as my spirit. Inside, my soul squawked that it's unfair—that I don't want to endure more months of PT—that my body robs me of what I *should* be doing—that no one else my age must worry about the existential and ethical questions I do. But I have trained myself to deal with emotions outside medical appointments and to focus on the prognosis. My physical therapist's angular jaw locked, awaiting my response to the vexing news. "So you're saying I'm a hip pop star?" is all I can think to reply. My pun puts his shoulders at ease.

My drooping body remains on the examination table as he explains an exhausting series of follow-ups. Words like "hip flexor," "quadriceps femoris," and "iliopsoas tendon" are scribbled in my notepad phonetically, me the secretary to my own pain.

My cane and I hobble to the car like exhaling after holding your breath too long underwater. One glimpse of my husband's tender eyes is all it takes to release the downpour of emotions I have shielded from my physical therapist in the exam room. In my frustration, I spurt, "I just—I just want to be *normal*."

Without hesitating, Andrew gently counters, "But you aren't normal. You're extraordinary."

Yes, even disabled people secretly yearn to be "normal" on days when it feels like our bodies let us down. We have so internalized the expectation that our bodies *should* function in a linear way that we can feel frustrated when they don't play along. It feels like pulling a "do not pass go, do not collect $200" card when everyone else is making bank. Especially being disabled from such a young age, it can feel like there are so many things I cannot do that my friends take for granted, so many things that are taken away from me—as if I was promised a life on foot. It can feel like I am robbed of the life I *should* be living, one full of blessed hashtags and overpriced lattes.

In that moment with my physical therapist, I certainly wished I had a "get out of jail free" card that could eliminate the months of additional physical therapy that followed. There's a reason I call PT "perpetual torture." It is not my idea of a good time. Grueling and everlasting, physical therapy is like that irritating song you can't get out of your head, but you never get beyond the incessant chorus. You spend all day trying to remember the words, but they never materialize beyond the most irritating lines. Physical therapy is exactly like that, with the added feature of feeling stabbed by burning knives while being informed that it's good for you to feel pain. That means it's working, they reassure me, eyes peering over their stopwatches. That Tuesday, I just wanted some assurance, a promissory note of sorts, that it would be worth it, that it would yield some tangible results. At the very least, I yearned for a set of rules that guaranteed a specific outcome. In my desperate desire to be "normal," I had forgotten that life is not a game of Monopoly. That no one can promise me a future physicality because one does not exist—not for me, not for anyone.

In those moments, disabled people need someone to remind us of who we really are: not a catalog of things we can't do or a calendar of disappointing medical appointments or even a race car jailed by a board game. We are a parade of extraordinary experiences that can teach the world about what it means to be embodied. Andrew reminds me when I momentarily forget: I am extraordinary. My pop hip and blue leg and spasmic nerves can't take that away. My body has proved more medical specialists wrong than right. My body is a marvel. It doesn't always feel like one, or even do what I desire, but my body is a gift, one that I am grateful for, crumpled wrapping paper included. I am proud to be disabled.

Having disability pride doesn't mean that there aren't difficult aspects of my disability or that I love it all the time. I am allowed to get frustrated, to feel down, to wonder about the complexity of my disabled body. I am allowed to be a full human, not an inspirational hashtag. Disability pride is simply declaring that my disability does not make me less of a human in any way. It proclaims that I am not an embarrassment.

We don't simply arrive at the destination of accepting ourselves as disabled. We must learn to embrace each part of our disabled bodies as a revolutionary act of believing that we are inherently worthy as image-bearers. The world and the church teach us that we are not enough, that we need to be "fixed" (read: cured) to be whole, that we have all the makings of a "before" picture of a prayer makeover. To go against these ingrained ideas is to reject a lifetime of conditioning about how our bodies are *supposed* to behave. I just need an occasional reminder that I am not who they say I am. That my disabled body is nothing to be ashamed of. That I, too, am extraordinary.

"Do you think we could hide your cane?" the school photographer requests. "Or maybe if we put you off to the side, people won't notice your scooter. What do you think? We want the photo to look *nice*." Translation: my body is too ugly to be featured in a snapshot anyone wants to display. Evidently, I come with a graphic content warning.

That afternoon, I drag my wilted limbs to another doctor's appointment where they poke and prod me like a piece of meat being trimmed. Another specialist recommends amputation in hushed tones without making eye contact. The medical gaze fixates on everything that's wrong with me and my rare body. Rare, they say, with judgment and embarrassment, almost as though it's an accusation. Rare, like I've won the genetic lottery, except not the one that anyone buys a ticket for. Not the one that makes me Gisele or Beyoncé or Idris Elba. Not the one that makes me beautiful.

"Don't let them take your leg. You want a chance of a *normal* life," person after person recommends without prompting. As if "normal" is the summation of one's life goals. What is "normal," anyway? My twelve-year-old self doesn't know it yet, but their ableism seeps into my pores and adheres to my brain waves. It won't be until I'm in my twenties, when I am told for the millionth time that someone "doesn't think of me as disabled," that I notice the sticky residue—when I find myself wondering why that's a compliment. Their ableism is a syrup I've internalized as I process why I'm trying to "overcome" being disabled. When I wonder why I instinctively hide my cane in photos.

But what if my body could be something other than a freak show or a rare disease? What if my body isn't a metaphor or a cautionary tale? Could I be . . . beautiful? Not my joyful smile or even my inspiring personality, but my emaciated leg. The one that has stopped growing hair or circulating blood. The one that has accumulated medical case files and perplexed specialists. The one that twitches without my consent. I brush off the thought because I am too sensible to want to be beautiful. I want to be smart, compassionate, and generous; I want to topple pharaohs and pillage empires so that everyone can flourish. But somewhere deep down, in a place I don't allow myself to visit often, I wish there was a category for my body to be something other than a blemish to crop out of a "nice" photo.

Maybe I could be Venus de Milo. Towering over her admirers at six feet, eight inches tall, the double amputee is a goddess, literally the embodiment of love and beauty. Her smug expression, sculpted abs, and flowing sarong add to her allure. She is dreamlike, mysterious, cunning, and domineering. She is beautiful. It's her disabled body that is beautiful. If she had arms, she'd be just another boring marble statue in the Louvre. But her disability makes her beautiful. If Picasso had painted realistic neoclassical portraits, he would be just another artist. His jagged lines and distorted figures reinvent the curvature expected in idealized paintings. His forms are innovative, shattered, kinetic, striking, and beautiful. It's his disabled bodies that are beautiful. Think of Frida Kahlo. Vincent van Gogh. Ángela de la Cruz. Paul Klee. Ada Limón. Francisco Goya. Maya Angelou. Henri Matisse. Yayoi Kusama. Amanda Gorman. Sins Invalid. And dozens of other disabled body-minds who have made beautiful art. Disability can be beautiful. If only we would notice the beauty it reveals to us.

Walking on legs is intermittent, clunky, full of sudden collisions with the unsuspecting concrete. I glide through the world, drumming on the pavement, harmonizing a soothing melody with the wheels of my scooter. No clumsy thumping or blundering across the uneven ground. I soar with consistency, ease, and grace. My cobalt cane strikes the pavement with fierce proclamation. "I am disabled, hear me roar," it declares to the world.

But how could I be beautiful when people perceive my body as ugly, lacking, and deficient? If you have a deficit lens, you will only ever interpret my body through what it cannot do: walk, climb stairs, wiggle toes. But what if you thought of me as Venus? If she had arms, she'd be just another monotonous sculpture amid a sea of Greek marble. It's her disability that *makes* her unique. What if you interpreted my body through the way it has repeatedly proved doctors wrong? What if you acknowledged that my body is a medical marvel? That underneath the radical treatments and abnormal gait is a tenacious spirit that cannot be confined? That these nerves tell a story much rarer than my rare disease?

Every time I rejoice in what I can do instead of what I cannot, every time I go out into the world without shame or embarrassment, every time I celebrate how my body is marvelous, I resist this core spiritual lie by declaring the truth: that all of us bear God's image to the world, not just those of us deemed "beautiful" or nondisabled. My disabled body reflects God's radiance. Sometimes we miss its sparkle because we're too caught up in my gadgets and popping joints to notice. But make no mistake: my disabled body is extraordinary.

The familiar ding of a text message comes through on a misty Wednesday at 7 p.m. My phone tells me the text is from a friend who's at an engagement party I am missing. I'm "out of spoons," I told her earlier, using our shorthand for when my body says nope. Folks in the disability and chronic pain communities use spoons as a metaphor to explain what it is like to live in a body with fluctuating limitations. Christine Miserandino pioneered spoon theory when she explained living with lupus to a friend.[1] Sitting at a diner, Miserandino grabbed a nearby stack of spoons to symbolize how each activity costs one "spoon" to a person with a chronic illness. Spoons represent the amount of energy used on each task. Referring to spoons keeps my message buoyant, so I don't emotionally hijack the night, but even responding to texts is taxing. Spoons give everyone an emotional off-ramp so they can carry on having a good time at the party without me.

I click on the screen, illuminating my face. It reads, "Sorry you feel a bit worn out. Hope you get some rest." My heart sinks deep below the center of gravity and somehow also rises to my throat like acid lingering after a spicy meal. I want to brush it off, but I am too irritated to be kind. Like that song you can't get out of your head that you don't even like. The fragmented lyrics play on repeat: "You feel a bit worn out, worn out, worn out. Hope you get some rest, rest, rest, resssssssst."

"A bit worn out," I think to myself. When I say I am out of spoons, I mean that my leg buckled, and my body collapsed on the way to the bathroom. I mean that my husband dressed

1. Christine Miserandino, "The Spoon Theory," *But You Don't Look Sick* (blog), 2003, https://butyoudontlooksick.com/articles/written-by-christine/the-spoon-theory.

me for bed, a bed that I did not leave for the next three days. I mean that the pain was so intense that my body shook without my consent. That my highly educated brain couldn't form sentences because the pain crashed over my frail body for so long that I short-circuited. That I understood in my gut why 70 percent of people who have this self-harm. I wish I was only a "bit worn out."

I consider sending all of that back, but I know I'll regret it when I'm in less of an agony-induced self-pity party. I recognize I have gone full English professor on her, unraveling the nuances of a mere few words in the text, probably sent while driving to the party, and I realize I am being unfair. I know that she loves me, that she didn't mean what I am making of it. I want her to understand my life, to know that spoons are a way to explain without getting into the whole temporary paralysis of it all. I want her to know that no amount of being tired and injecting double-shot venti lattes into her veins will make her grasp what it's like to be in my body. I want to be missed at a party I can't attend because of a body I didn't choose.

Some days I rest, and I still have no spoons. Some days I might have twelve spoons, whereas other days I have five. Some days I am so low on spoons that I don't give a fork.

I want to unravel all this to my friend, but I know the middle of an engagement party is not the time. But when is, I wonder to myself? If I tell people what my body is like, if I try to help them understand even a sliver of it, I end up confirming a lot of their assumptions about disability: that our lives are depressing tales of stuff we can't do. If I use my code of spoons, I (unintentionally) dismiss the severity of my own pain. Did I bring this on myself? I second-guess using the spoons code. Maybe I encourage cavalier responses by using coded language. Spoons are a way to feel less alone, but somehow, I still feel alone.

This is what it is like to talk to disability allies. We want them to understand, but we know that they do not, maybe even cannot. We use inside jokes and coded cutlery, but we wonder whether they realize how things really are behind the mask. We are silenced when we try to tell our stories, sometimes from our own fear that if we let people in on our pain, they'll use it against us as proof that our lives were never worth living anyway. We are erased from a society that never wanted us around, and sometimes by our own text messages, because it is too fraught to explain the complexity of our lives.

We are stuck.

Even in writing this book I fear my relationship with my disability will be misunderstood. I worry that the one story people will remember will be this one, or the one where I am frustrated that my life is not "normal." I fear that people will pity me, feel sorry for me, be (even more) awkward around me. Like a pet-adoption video playing on your emotions with a weepy ballad aimed right at your fragile heart. If you hear the piano of a Sarah McLachlan song, get out now. I fear that people will go so far into the land of celebrating disability that they will forget about any of the difficult parts of it. It will become another version of prosperity gospel. Instead of praising health and wealth, we'll pretend disability is all smiles with no space for suffering.

The truth is that being disabled is hard, beautiful, heartbreaking, illuminating, full of loss, and full of life. I am grateful I am disabled, and yet I wouldn't wish it on anyone. My body is a menace and a marvel. I am proud to be disabled, but it is not the sum of who I am. The hardest part of being disabled isn't the pain, it's the people. It's trying to explain. It's asking people to rethink all their assumptions in text messages. It's being bombarded with slurs about me every day that no one seems to think are a big deal. It's getting up the courage to share my pain with someone, only for it to be dismissed by comparison. (No, my disability is not like that time you broke your ankle in junior high.) It's having to weigh the pros and cons of sharing any of this with someone, risking the relationship, knowing they might roll their eyes at my frustration. Or, worse, just distance themselves because I am too messy. It's worrying that I am not really missed at the party, because people would rather not have my spoonie baggage around anyway. The hardest part isn't the pain, it's the people. But I hope that one day it will be the pain.

And yes, I did eventually share all this with my texting friend. She responded with grace and kindness, despite my hyper-analysis of a few scattered texts. I am glad I risked confiding in her. She gives me hope that perhaps the pain being the worst part is within reach. If only more people could have her willing-ness to listen, to learn, to love. She is who I remember when others forget about me. She is the example that disability allies are worth investing in. She is the hope that people can change.

When I first became disabled, I fought with my body. I wanted to force myself to remain productive. I didn't want anyone to think that I was lazy. I knew that if I worked twice as hard, I could convince everyone around me that nothing had changed. Sure, I couldn't walk, but I was still *me*: the type A know-it-all who never encountered a test she couldn't ace. But my body had other plans. She forced me to take breaks, slow down, and rest. She forced me to live by spoons.

The ever-fluctuating spoon allotment is irksome to explain to folks outside the spoonie community. It doesn't always make sense why on one day we have more spoons than on others. Some days my husband helps me put my socks on, always to the chorus of me telling him he "knocks my socks off." Other days I can whizz through a to-do list faster than Leslie Knope.

Every day is a series of microdecisions about where to spend the finite spoons. Spoonies are in a constant negotiation with our bodies about what we can do on any given day. We don't come with spoon-o-meters on our hips. (Wouldn't that be rad if we did, though?) It is a process of learning, failing, and relearning that gives us insight into how many spoons we have on any given Monday. We always count spoons to make sure we don't go over our ration for the day, because we cannot get any more. If we are out of spoons, we crash. There is no silverware drawer for us. We cannot save our spoons for ladle. We cannot borrow from tomorrow's spoons today.

It's not like a boot camp for spoonies. You can't push past the limits of what you *thought* was possible only to discover you are capable of infinitely more than you imagined. We are not a Gatorade commercial. There is no perceived wall that you can push through with the right number of electrolytes, caffeine, or motivational speeches to get to the other side. There is a wall that slams you in the face, and—more often than not—it is closer than it appears.

Last time I ran out of spoons, I did not leave my bed, let alone the house, for three days, Jesus-in-the-tomb-style. I lay prostrate, sitting up only to eat or go to the bathroom. When I finally reemerged from my cocoon, announcing "I have risen!" my body was frail and trembled with the smallest of tasks. I had to move at a pace so slow that sloths would have beat me in a race. Running out of spoons cuts like a knife.

God is a fan of spoons. In making the covenant with the Israelites, God commands, "Remember the sabbath day, and keep it holy. Six days you shall labor and do all your work. But the seventh day is a sabbath to the LORD your God" (Exod. 20:8–10). Most of us give that a "sure, Jan," and move on with our lives. We use every justification in the book to avoid the Sabbath: Times were different back then. The Israelites didn't have *my* boss! Sabbath isn't going to pay the rent. Phew, Jesus came to fulfill the law.

We forget that rest is good for us. Rhythms of rest help our bodies and minds rejuvenate. Regular rest reduces stress, shrinks the risk of heart disease, boosts our immune system, and deepens our creativity. Study after study confirms what we already know: rest is exactly what the Great Physician ordered.

Taking sabbath is a disabled practice. It declares to the world that we are worthy not because we checked items off a to-do list, but because we are image-bearers. It allows us to rest, breathe, and rejuvenate. It offers a counter-practice to the competition of our capitalistic world pushing us to be harder, better, faster, stronger. (Try as we might, we are not a Daft Punk song.) It declares that the turbocharged pace of trying to outpace one another is not healthy or necessary for abundant life. It follows the rhythms of creation in rooting, reaping, and releasing. It allows our bodies to be connected to the breath of life, the womb of time, and the sacredness of all creation.

Sabbath is a formative practice that requires an act of faith. Sabbath declares what spoonies know to be true: we are not in control of our bodies, and all bodies have fluctuating needs. Practicing sabbath compels us to acknowledge that truth in some way. It requires that we affirm that the work left undone will be tomorrow's worry. That you are faithful enough or just exhausted enough to turn off the fretting and instead rejuvenate. Sabbath is at the core of disability justice principles because it affirms that all are worthy simply because we are made in the image of God. We cannot win or lose our divine worth.

Nondisabled people can learn from spoonies by developing regular rhythms of rest. Some days I rest, and I still have no spoons. Spoonies cannot inject ourselves with a liquid spoon no matter how much caffeine we inhale. But we do know how to let our bodies—not our calendars or clocks or careers—dictate where we spend our energy. Spoons are a precious resource for us, so we must use them wisely. Observing sabbath is not going to solve a shortage of spoons, but it can give nondisabled folks a small glimpse of the rest required to live by spoons.

Sabbath, shabbat, and spoon theory are all embodied practices asking folks to incorporate rest into the rhythms of our routines. No matter how sci-fi movies try to convince us otherwise, the body is not a machine. We cannot always be rehabilitated by replacing the right parts or receiving a tune-up. Your car breaks? Take it to the mechanic. After draining your time and wallet, you drive home with your car repaired, no longer sounding like a fork stuck in a blender. When it breaks down, fixing it is as simple as swapping out the carburetor. The body isn't like that. Medicine and bio-capitalism lure us into believing that the body can be reduced to a series of replaceable parts. That's not how bodies work.

Bodies are like gardens. We can put the right ingredients in the soil. We can tend to them and cultivate growth in various ways. But the ultimate success of the crop isn't up to us. It is dependent on the temperature, water, humidity, and sunlight, all of which are out of our control. Our damaged organs or limbs cannot be replaced like a snapped fan belt. Sometimes we do all the "right" things—eat nourishing foods, exercise, reduce stress—and yet there are parts of our bodies that are not normative. No amount of eating kale or using heat lamps will change the fact that I am disabled.

We need to recast our bodies as gardens and not as machines. If we do, we might learn the practice of spoonies. We know that gardens change with the seasons and require regular rest in order to restore the land. Our bodies, too, need respite and recharge, not just quick repair and replacement parts. Our bodies are worthy of rest.

In my closet rests a mirror, glued to the side of a bleached foam-core box that I sit in front of in the afternoon. When I place my left leg in the box, the mirror on the outside reflects the image of my right leg to my brain, tricking it into believing both legs are capable of enduring touch, movement, and stimulation.

I watch as my left leg transforms into my right. My gaze remains fastened to the mirror as I touch my ankle with various textures: the coarse grains of sandpaper, the prickly bristles of a cone brush, the silky cucumber mesh of a loofah, the tickling caress of a feather, the cooling gel of putty, among others.

I take the mirror box with me to the neurologist's office, where she coaches me, "The trick is to turn off the part of your brain that thinks." "Hold up, there's a part of my brain that doesn't think?" I inwardly fret. Unease creeps in; my cheeks redden with confusion about the corners of my mind. "How—how do you recommend I turn off thinking?" My voice trembles, betraying my uncertainty. "Do I have an 'off' switch I don't know about?" We both break into chuckles that resemble a work laugh at a dad joke. (I still don't know the answer.)

It is week three of my neuroplasticity training, and I remain uncertain about the entire endeavor. I have read the pamphlets, done all the research. I watched a video that compared our brains to Jell-O, wiggling around in our skulls awaiting a new mold to (re)shape them, like a mood ring for our pliable brains. Too bad I avoid Jell-O at every potluck. I prefer my food not to jiggle.

The basic premise of neuroplasticity training is that we can rewire our brains through deliberate coaching, much like athletes develop muscle mass for competitive sports. Inside our skulls, our Jell-O's hard drive contains a petabyte of data. That's bigger than the total storage capacity of Netflix. Turns out you *can't* fill your brain binge-watching, even if you watched all that Netflix has to offer. Our brains' hard drives are massive.

So massive, in fact, that our brains don't waste brain power on activities we do every day. Experiences, memory, and actions all carve out pathways in the brain that are strengthened via repetition. Our brains learn these routes as shortcuts for actions we take all the time. Brain waves travel down an entrenched pathway instead of forging their own route. We run on autopilot. Usually we call this "muscle memory," but it might be more accurate to call it a subconscious etching into our brains to make us more energy efficient. It's the reason we can tie our shoelaces without singing the song, input our phone's password without verbalizing it, or drive home from work without really remembering that we've done it. Habits are helpful. They are the brain's way of conserving energy. Thanks, brain.

But what happens when you keep traveling down that pathway after it becomes unhealthy? Habits can also be harmful. Yes, we are still watching, Netflix. It's hard to stop. We do it without consciously thinking. We get stuck in the binge. Brains take the path of least resistance because energy is required to carve a new path. Just try brushing your teeth with your nondominant hand or forging someone else's signature. It's disorienting when your Jell-O morphs to sculpt a new track. It feels squidgy.

For me, neuroplasticity means teaching my brain that not every sensation is excruciating. My brain is one smart cookie. She has learned that anything—even a delicate sheet—touching my left side is agonizing, so she avoids it at all costs. "Ow," she shrieks, shriveling in response to any sensation. A sheet, a cleat, a sock, a rock: my leg does not like to be touched with a feather in any weather. Pain, I am.

The idea behind neuroplasticity training is to reeducate my brain to interpret sensations and textures *other* than pain. Instead of putting my left side through torture, I am coached to touch my right leg with assorted objects, all while observing in the mirror box. The magic mirror will trick my brain into believing she is watching my left leg and rewire my Jell-O circuit board. I'll be two right legs and a new brain before we know it. Maybe my nervous system can be my ally and not my enemy. That's the idea.

After learning it has worked for wounded warriors, I agree to give it a try. Reluctantly. I assure myself it is low risk with a potentially high reward. At worst, I am playing footsie with a mirror. At best, I can rewire my entire brain. My dad assembles a bespoke mirror box with the dimensions of my leg so that I have a higher likelihood of believing the illusion is "real." Meanwhile, my mum produces dozens of distinctive textures, each in my favorite hue of teal, to make me grin while mutating my mind from the inside out.

And so, the work begins. It is weird, remapping your brain. It feels like observing yourself get stitches while under anesthesia or watching a video of yourself petting a kangaroo when you were too young to remember. You know it's real, and yet it *feels* fabricated. "Eerie" is the word I'd use. I drill myself to trust my eyes, but I'm not sure my brain believes me. In the research phase, I had cross-examined the neurologist about whether there was any chance of rewiring something I didn't want changed, like my memories. "We don't think so," was the high-pitched, not-so-reassuring response. "So, you're telling me there's a chance!" flashes into my mind from *Dumb and Dumber*.

Desperate to cling to my warm fuzzies, I remove my polar-bear slippers, gingerly place my ankle inside the box, and stare into the mirror. Nothing happens. Nothing except wishing I'd had time to paint my toenails a vibrant coral to offset the frigid hue of my mottled skin. My mind wanders to pressing subjects like "How would I hide a giraffe in New York City?" and "What's the opposite of a koala?"

Bewildered, uncanny, and tentative, I scold myself to stay on task. It's disorienting gazing at your own ankle with such intensity, without flinching, for so long. It's like being confronted with an unflattering selfie where you can't filter out your forced smile no matter how many times you hit the yellow magic wand. You focus on every detail, every blemish. Suddenly I notice the surgery scars and entangled roots of my veins. I feel gooey. But I keep at it because persistence is the name of the game.

Does it work? I don't know. Some days I'm persuaded I'm wasting my time with a placebo effect. "Oh yeah, it works!" I reassure myself, before fretting that I've sipped too much of the neuroplasticity Kool-Aid. Other days, I look down and wonder whether I've started to internalize the training. Working or not, neuroplasticity training sessions are some of the least torturous treatments I've ever had. And I find myself wondering whether this is what our spiritual formation is like.

Neuroplasticity allows you to believe you are not the worst retort you've said in a fight or that flippant financial gaffe from twenty years ago that still embarrasses you. Our brains have morphed into another shape entirely. Remember the Jell-O mold? We are constantly changing. Physiologically, we are not the same people we once were. In fact, we have more in common with our peers than we do with our two-year-old selves; we just share the same origin story with that precocious, kangaroo-petting kid. Neuroplasticity training recognizes that we are not just what happens to us but how we choose to think about what happens to us. There is so much that is out of our control, but we can change how we think about what happens to us. I cannot control the fact that my nervous system translates touch into torment, but I can change how I think about the sensations. Neuroplasticity training declares that it is possible to redeem even the most painful parts of our stories. It believes that we don't have to live in the wake of our shame.

We like to pretend that being an adult means never trying anything new or appearing foolish, as if we leave that feeling behind in our childhoods. We think we can outgrow the need to be vulnerable. Our careers, our hobbies, our ministries, and our lives are built on doing what we are good at, successful at, gifted at—to inoculate ourselves from any potential embarrassment at failure or foolishness. But neuroplasticity training means trying, failing, and trying again. Rebuilding your brain means looking foolish. It means staring at your ankle in a mirror as you touch it with a random hodgepodge of unrelated objects, hoping it will transform your neuropathways. It means showing up, being present, and doing the work, even when you don't always notice the results. It means believing that you can change.

We are new creations, able to shed who we once were by retraining our brains that our past selves are not who we need to be (2 Cor. 5:17). We "have the mind of Christ" (1 Cor. 2:16). We are "transformed by the renewing of [our] minds" (Rom. 12:2). We are called to "set [our] minds on things that are above, not on things that are on earth" (Col. 3:2). We are to think about "whatever is true, whatever is honorable, whatever is just, whatever is pure, whatever is pleasing, whatever is commendable, if there is any excellence and . . . anything worthy of praise" (Phil. 4:8). Isn't that what neuroplasticity training is all about? It's refocusing the body-mind to be transformed into something not of this world. It's choosing to flip the script when it comes to what we tell ourselves *about* ourselves.

This is not the power of positive thinking. It's not patting ourselves on the back, letting Jesus take the wheel, or listening to motivational speeches full of toxic positivity. There are indeed disabilities aside from bad attitudes, and some days do have bad vibes. It's not overconfidence or fake it until you make it. Nor does it diminish the real agony that people experience with depression, anxiety, addiction, and trauma. Neuroplasticity doesn't change the fact that I am disabled. It cannot erase the ways our bodies keep score simply by thinking about something else. It's a process. Neuroplasticity allows us to respond to the lies of shame with the truth of new creation. It declares what is true, that we have eternal worth, even if we haven't fully experienced this truth yet. It is the belief that we can participate in creating a new pathway where the old one was destructive. It is the now and not yet. It is the promise of new creation that we believe in our bones but have not yet breathed through our lungs. It is the declaration that death has no sting for resurrection people, but we sit with its sorrow anyway.

Sometimes, when we talk about spiritual formation, we want a church camp high with all our troubles melting away. That might be comforting, but it's not sustainable. Spiritual formation is not all golden retriever puppies and fuzzy socks. Spiritual formation should not try to minimize the trauma our body-minds have endured. It should be holistic and include the gritty realities of our aching lives. Our faith can be like our brains: living, dynamic, elastic, and malleable. We are instructed to "take every thought captive to obey Christ" as if wrestling harmful practices away from ourselves (2 Cor. 10:5). Maybe taking every thought captive means measuring your rogue thoughts against what you know to be true instead of against what you have been taught to believe about yourself. Maybe it means reminding yourself that you, just as you are, are divine because you are made in the Creator's radiant image. Maybe it means practicing neuroplasticity training.

In the mirror, I compare my foot's reaction to what I know to be true. Loofas are not vicious. Feathers should not frighten. Touch is not always torturous. And maybe one day, my left leg—and my sympathetic nervous system—will believe it too. In the interim, I sit, I wait, and I hope against hope that it means something other than playing mirror footsie. And if it doesn't, then at least I'm willing to risk setting my mind on the things above. At least I am willing to value my body-mind as worthy of investment. At least I am willing to practice resurrection.

We are resurrection people. We believe that the dead pathways of our lives can be rejuvenated to bring forth new life. Some days practicing resurrection and becoming a new creation looks like thinking outside the (mirror) box.

REFLECTION AND RESPONSE

▶ Learn about disabled people throughout history. Choose a disabled person (such as Frida Kahlo, Harriet Tubman, Judy Heumann, or Fannie Lou Hamer) and learn more about their life and experience with disability.

▶ Read, listen, and learn from disabled people about the world today. A great place to start is Alice Wong's *Disability Visibility* podcast or edited collection, *Disability Visibility: First-Person Stories from the Twenty-First Century* (New York: Vintage, 2020). Discuss what you learn with your friends, small group, or church community.

▶ Reflect. How might neuroplasticity training help you reroute some of your (unfruitful) habits? Choose one task to try to relearn this week. Start small, like brushing your teeth with your nondominant hand or taking an alternative route to somewhere you go regularly. How did relearning make you feel? What can you learn from disabled people in your community that you have not been open to learning before?

TOP TEN
Disability Icebreakers

Folks say these when I am approaching in my mobility scooter. Usually, they are strangers. Always, they are awkward. Disability is not an icebreaker, a pickup line, or a way to create shared laughter for nondisabled people.

10. "Wide load, everyone. Make way! Stand aside! Look out, roadrunner coming through!"

9. Any time I stand or reach out of my wheelchair: "It's a miracle!" Or, during December: "It's a *Christmas* miracle!"

8. "Don't run me over now!"

7. "Do you have a license for that thing?"

6. "But you don't look like you need that thing."

5. "Wow, you're in a wheelchair!"

4. "Here comes Professor X!"

3. "Good for you for getting out and about."

2. "It must be nice to sit down all day."

1. "What's wrong with you?"

Disabled Foundations

Jostling as we climb to the bonfire, my teenage body clings to his broad shoulders as he carries me up the winding dirt stairs to a worship night beneath the sequoias. Dust sticks to the sweat of his linebacker neck as we ascend toward the acoustic guitar music for almost half a mile. Me, jolting up and down while the aroma of smoke dances beneath my nostrils. Him, wheezing louder the farther we climb. My main goal is trying not to slip off, but I am suddenly overly attentive to every pound of my drooping body. "Maybe I shouldn't have eaten that second scoop of mint chip last night," I ponder to myself as I melt into his tense back.

People from my church take turns piggybacking me while we're on this mountain retreat. I am passed around like a white elephant gift no one has the courage to throw away. More than one person makes the joke that we are "carrying one another's burdens." Only this time the burden is my body. I am everybody's inspiration, but nobody's friend.

They have a deep commitment to inclusion, they promise me. They want to make sure I'm not left behind in my wheelchair. There's even a joke about those tacky apocalyptic books and not being raptured while at Christian camp. It never occurs to anyone that everything the camp features—from a zip line to an obstacle course, fire pits to amphitheaters, and something affectionally known as "the blob," an inflatable device that launches people into the lake—has been manufactured. Even the lake is human-made. It just hasn't been made to include me.

"God doesn't see you as disabled," they reassure me.

"Sign up to use the new prayer room," we're encouraged one chilly Sunday morning at a different church. No one bothers to mention whether the space is ADA-compliant. It isn't. When we get there, we must traverse gravel, the notorious nemesis of the disability community, before climbing fourteen steep wooden steps. My husband lugs me up the staircase, me joking with him to go faster the whole way, him chuckling and almost slipping on the slick incline. A vaulted room awaits us, adorned with fuzzy pillows, a plush rug, and warm-glowing string lights. Cozy emanates everywhere. Every inch of the space has been lovingly curated for comfort, where people feel safe to divulge the deepest parts of themselves. It is undeniably intimate. Earth tones, fleece throws, and flickering candles wrap you in a warm embrace as you sit in the butterfly chair and read calligraphed Bible verses on the walls. It is beautiful.

Without my husband hoisting me to the top, I couldn't participate. I know this is unintentional, forgotten even; no one is trying to exclude me. But that's the problem. No one has bothered to be intentional at all. While spending ample time, money, and creativity on this inviting space, no one considered whether it was truly inviting to all bodies. Perhaps instead of purchasing vintage pine furniture and curating rustic decor, the focus should have been on including people—people like me. I shouldn't require my husband's brawn to access a prayer room.

"God doesn't see you as disabled," they reassure me.

The building we are meeting in has no ramp. Three slight concrete stairs are all that prevent me from entering. Most Sundays, we can manage to heave my body over the threshold and into the dank, dilapidated theater where we gather. Many Sundays, it costs me so many spoons that I can't do much else. I don't want to stir up trouble, but the cost of discipleship shouldn't be spoons for service.

When we move to a new building across town, I am relieved to learn it includes a ramp. And not just *any* ramp. A ramp wide enough for motorized four-wheelers, with an automatic door greeting me at the top. I am living the accessible dream! That is, until the church announces that our main entrance will be the one with ten stairs on either side of a split staircase leading up to the Gothic revival building.

What's the big deal? I still made it into the building, and this time with a ramp. The life of the church—announcements, coffee, and community—took place on those steps, without me. Meanwhile, I was relegated to the side ramp, like a dirty little secret you're too embarrassed to greet at the front door. Why can't we all arrive through the entrance that is accessible? Ramps are for more than disabled folks. They ease access for strollers, seniors, and sound equipment just as much as wheelies. We are the gateway to creating a space that is accessible for everybody.

"God doesn't see you as disabled," they reassure me.

Everyone is quick to speak for God. God doesn't see me as disabled, yet communities gathered in God's name disable me from fully participating. When a group of nondisabled people make all the decisions for a community, they unwittingly perpetuate practices that exclude disabled people. This is not deliberate or vindictive. We are more often neglected than barred.

Most nondisabled people haven't given disability access much thought. Yet it has ramifications for everything from physical space to gathering etiquette, liturgy to song choice, theology to exegesis, and all aspects of community care.

How, when, and where we gather as a church can exclude, even if we aren't intending to reject anyone. I know no one intended any harm in all the examples that begin this chapter. No one meant for me to be excluded, but that didn't prevent me from being physically excluded. Architecture conveys meaning. You know in your gut when a film is set in New York City, even without anyone announcing it. The looming Manhattan sky-scrapers, the art deco scales of the Chrysler Building, the green robe garnishing Lady Liberty. New York City architecture is iconic, instantly recognizable regardless of whether you've vis-ited the city that never sleeps. Architecture conjures memories, transports us to a different time and space, and comforts us.

Physical space reveals who the world is built for and who we expect to use it. When pulpits are tall, ominous, and imposing, accessible only through a stairway to heaven, we're suggesting that a little person or a wheelchair user doesn't preach. We sim-ply *receive*. This might feel like a petty thing to you, but it reveals who we expect to lead and who we expect is only able to follow.

In the disability community, we talk about the need to bake disability inclusion in from the outset because it too often goes unnoticed by well-meaning nondisabled people. It's the blue-berries in blueberry muffins, we often say: it can't be added in later.[1] Otherwise, disabled people are easily discarded whenever cost and convenience are in the mix. If we must wait for money to become available before disabled people's needs are met, we may never be included. When we fool ourselves into believing we can include disabled people only out of guilt or charity,

---

1. Cordelia McGee-Tubb, "Baking Accessibility In," Clarity Conference, San Francisco, California, April 1, 2016, https://www.clarityconf.com/session/baking -accessibility-in.

we can easily abandon that practice in tough times, or when a more "deserving" cause comes along.[2] Instead, we need to think about disability inclusion not as charity but as faithfulness to the way of Jesus.

Accessibility is not just a checklist but an ethos. Sixty-inch-diameter toilet stalls and closed-captioning should be available, to be sure, but that is simply allowing disabled people to attend your church gatherings. We should go beyond the checklist mentality of patting ourselves on the back for the bare minimum, and instead think about how we can practice accessibility as much as possible.

We need to stop making excuses for disenfranchising or ignoring one-fourth of image-bearers from our churches. Cost, convenience, and ignorance are not reasons to exclude. We are made in the image of a Creator who breathed life into the mantis shrimp and the woolly mammoth, the purple-striped jellyfish and the jumping kangaroo, the sparklemuffin peacock spider and the Amazonian royal flycatcher. Surely, we, who are made in the image of such a Creator, can come up with an innovative solution to a narrow bathroom stall or staired entry. Beholding such a canvas of wild and wacky wildlife should fuel our imaginations for how to create accessibility in our church spaces. We can be more creative than we have been.

Accessibility is a point of departure, not a destination. We must assess and reassess the access needs of disabled folks in our community and make changes accordingly. This takes time, commitment, and creativity. There is not a one-size-fits-all model of accessibility, and it cannot be achieved overnight. It will require hard and enduring work. Some will fight you on it. Some will dismiss it. It will cost you friendships and time and money. It will be demanding and frustrating. It will cause

2. Bethany McKinney Fox makes a similar point in *Disability and the Way of Jesus: Holistic Healing in the Gospels and the Church* (Downers Grove, IL: IVP Academic, 2019), 186.

derision in ways you could never imagine. Some days you might even question whether it is worth it. But deep down, inside the place where your bones ache, you will know the truth. No amount of naysayers or pulled tithe or snide critiques can deny what you know to be true: disabled people are image-bearers, and we are always worth the cost of inclusion.

We need to crip our church spaces and practices. In the disability community, we talk about the need to crip spaces to reclaim a derogatory word that was crafted to mock our bodily difference. It signals that we shouldn't settle for "no ableism" or even for inclusion; we want to foster belonging. We don't just want disabled people to be invited to the table, we want to be such a core part of the group that we are missed when we are not around. We want to be able to be our full selves, not reduced to the label of disability. To crip something is to invite the way disability disrupts our ideas of what is normal and allow disability to lead how we gather and participate in a communal space without hierarchy.[3] Crip space is created by and for disabled people's needs. It centers the needs of disabled people and cultivates the environment and its norms with us in mind. Instead of adding us in as an afterthought, crip space considers our needs from the outset. It makes the muffins with the blueberries in the batter instead of tossing them on top after the muffins are baked.

Crip space cherishes people just as they are—crutches, chemical sensitivities, and all. It does not value humans for productivity or contributions, but instead celebrates each image-bearer as sacred. It gets creative in making spaces accessible and inclusive by drawing on the diverse gifts of the community. It understands that each human is worth the effort it takes to make a space accessible. It does not keep a record of costs when adding a

3. s.e. smith, "The Beauty of Spaces Created for and by Disabled People," *Catapult Magazine*, October 22, 2018, https://catapult.co/stories/the-beauty-of-spaces-created-for-and-by-disabled-people.

ramp or hiring an ASL interpreter, but instead protects disabled people as inherently worthy. It does not boast about how accessible it is, nor does it delight in being more inclusive than other churches. Crip space trusts disabled people when they courageously ask for what they need. It hopes that all spaces can transform to welcome even more image-bearers. It perseveres in its pursuit of inclusivity, no matter how long it takes or how impossible it seems to achieve. Crip space is loving our disabled neighbors. Crip space is the second greatest commandment in action. Crip space is love.

Crip space is more than just the physical space. It is a disability justice ethos that Christian communities can embody. It does not judge or mock when plans dissipate or goals aren't met due to a lack of spoons or bodily demands. It has the reassuring laughter of an inside joke, understanding what it's like to live in a body-mind outside the norm. It doesn't require an explanation for why, but simply sits in knowing silence with you. It does not try to fix but remains present, even when doing so is awkward and messy and uncomfortable. It refuses to hide from the agony, acknowledging that it is okay to not be okay. It does not seek answers or even words but communicates through the groans too deep to utter, groans that value the lived experience of a disabled body.

If you've ever been to a DeafSpace, you might have experienced how crip space can function. DeafSpace is built around Deaf culture and communication styles to allow people to communicate with one another in varied formats in a flexible and movable space. As many d/Deaf people will tell you, d/Deafness is a culture, not a disability. Terrible lighting, narrow sidewalks, and sharp angles limit sightlines, straining communication via ASL. DeafSpace is designed to minimize eye fatigue. Proximity, sensory reach, lights and color, and mobility are all principles of design for DeafSpace in order to create an atmosphere where d/Deaf people can communicate with ease.[4] Wide entrances and exits allow for signed conversations. Circular tables and chairs are (re)arranged so people can see one another. Limited backlight and glare increase visibility. DeafSpace is designed by and for d/Deaf people.

Instead of building a space centered on nondisabled people, churches can create spaces with and for disabled people. Deaf-Space provides an example of how this can function, but there are many ways to set up crip space that churches can cultivate. Disabled people in your community are already experts in what accommodations your church space needs. If they share what changes can make the community more inclusive to disabled people, don't waste time arguing or proving them wrong. Don't second-guess whether their experience is "right." Be eager to follow the lead of disabled people who are willing to do the heavy emotional labor of educating nondisabled people about our access needs. Crip space celebrates disability as a cultural identity, not just a physical impairment. It embraces disability knowledge and attempts to learn from it. It uses architecture to facilitate inclusivity instead of expecting disabled people to accept fickle or feeble accommodations. It changes the physical space to meet the needs of people rather than forcing disabled people to bend to the space. It recognizes that disability confers community—one where all bodies can thrive regardless of shifting abilities, because we have the tools to change the architecture and ethos of the space. Disability teaches us that our worth is not derived from our work or excellence or beauty, but from the humbling fact that we are image-bearers.

We need to crip the body of Christ to liberate us from settling for inclusion when we could invite people to fully belong. We need to build with and for disabled people so we

4. "DeafSpace," Gallaudet University, accessed May 18, 2021, https://www.gallaudet.edu/campus-design-and-planning/deafspace.

can foster mutual flourishing for disabled and nondisabled people alike.

God promises to crip new creation by building it around disabled people. Zechariah's depiction of Jerusalem's marvelous future includes this image: "Men and women of ripe old age will sit in the streets of Jerusalem, each of them with cane in hand because of their age. The city streets will be filled with boys and girls playing there" (Zech. 8:4–5 NIV). Disability is represented as natural as children playing in the streets, almost like a sitcom family montage. The elderly women and men are portrayed positively with their canes, without any sense that physical alteration must occur for Jerusalem to be restored. Jeremiah's vision for the restoration of Jerusalem shows God gathering disregarded people, including "the blind and the lame, expectant mothers and women in labor" to a restored city where God "will lead them beside streams of water on a level path where they will not stumble" (Jer. 31:8–9 NIV). The lame, the blind, those pregnant and in labor, the elderly, and children collectively offer a sign of hope for the restoration of the future. They remind the audience that they will not always be exiles and outcasts.

I imagine this stumble-free path as a type of divine access, traversing the inhospitable terrain to build a more accessible incline in its place. Jeremiah groups "the lame" together with pregnancy, and Zechariah with children, both desired and positive associations in the ancient world. There is no mention of God curing blindness or lameness. Instead, God incorporates folks into the beloved community by meeting their access needs. This future welcomes us just as we are, leading us on paths that accommodate our physical needs rather than attempting to fix us before we are permitted entrance to the kingdom. It reminds us that the vibrant goodness between us can be restored.

This image of a restored Jerusalem is similar to the instructions given in Hebrews for how to follow Jesus: "'Make level paths for your feet,' so that the lame may not be disabled, but rather healed" (Heb. 12:13 NIV). God redeems the dismissive value of "the lame" by building the community around them and encouraging us to do the same. Regardless of whether I am lame, I should not be disabled by the church's inaccessible buildings, practices, or prayers.

We often think of healing as running marathons in super-fit bodies, but in Israel's story, limping becomes a mark of relational interdependence. When Jacob receives his new name, he learns to walk with a limp because of his wrestling blessing; in doing so, he symbolizes Israel perpetually learning the interdependence of disability. Limping becomes a way of moving beyond the self-sufficient hustle to define self-worth through independent prosperity and into the reality where we all help facilitate one another's thriving if we accept our human limits. Just like nondisabled people today, Israel is constantly trying to define itself as people who do not need God. They want to create their own way in the world, to outpace the need for God. But God doesn't seem interested in our self-improvement projects or independence. God is more invested in our transformation into mutual thriving throughout the community of creation. Relational interdependence is always the goal. We are not trying to get to a point of stability where we don't need God or the beloved community. Disabled people already know this truth well because our lives are beautiful portraits of interdependent flourishing.

When describing restoration in the days to come, Scripture often returns to the image of a lame Israel as a remnant. In Micah, God claims, "I will assemble the lame and gather those who have been driven away, and those whom I have afflicted. The lame I will make the remnant, and those who were cast off, a strong nation; and the Lord will reign over them in

Mount Zion now and forevermore" (Mic. 4:6–7). Similarly, in Zephaniah, God promises, "I will deal with all your oppressors at that time. And I will save the lame and gather the outcast, and I will change their shame into praise and renown in all the earth" (Zeph. 3:19).

In both passages, lameness describes the remnant, the purest of the pure, the faithful few, who remained loyal despite exile. Only this remnant of Jacob will return. Babylon, by contrast, has no remnant. The lame exiles are God's assurance that the entire people group will not be destroyed. They are promised a future flourishing outside the current state of oppression. As Walter Brueggemann notices, "Members of the remnant community have no investment in the present world and not only do they not benefit from the system, but they are glad to see it go, given their deep confidence that Yahweh will have for them a better future."[5] They realize that their allegiance is to God even in the midst of exile, because they are not at home in the current world. Disabled people are the prophetic witness that even their exile will be redeemed for God's glory.

Some might imagine that the vindication of the lame exiles will include wind sprints with boundless energy, but perhaps it is more accurate to say that in their lameness, the remnant become the faction of people who are still dependent on the living God. Limping is the way to faith, then, because it requires a trust and dependency on God and the beloved community, instead of your own independent strength.

Perhaps those of us who are already lame continue to act as a remnant because we have learned this interdependence. We know that we are more than what our bodies can produce, and we have escaped from the myth that we are reliant on our bodies to find joy and fulfillment. We are the faithful few who

---

5. Walter Brueggemann, *An Introduction to the Old Testament: The Canon and Christian Imagination* (Louisville: Westminster John Knox, 1989).

know what the interdependence of faith feels like, and it feels like a limp.

For one who "doesn't see me as disabled," God sure focuses on the lame when giving us glimpses of new creation and restoration. God doesn't remake bodies to fit the world but restores the world to welcome our diverse bodies. God's kingdom is built around disabled people, and so, too, should our churches, as they are appetizers for the banquet of the kingdom. This kingdom isn't like our ranked structures, but a kin-dom: a place where interdependence and relational ties supersede any hierarchy.[6] Disabled people have an embodied way of being in the world that punctures the illusion of certainty and normalcy. We live in the gap between the now and not yet. In our lives, nothing is certain, and there is no reliable routine or assured future. We are liberated from the bondage of constantly striving to prove our self-worth and can help teach the church the valuable lessons that our body-minds have taught us. "The lame" can act as the foundation of the new kingdom if we reimagine the blessing of disability in our communities and are willing to learn from it.

This is how I imagine crip space: with "the lame" as a remnant. Build *with* us. Build alongside us. Create space for us to thrive. Then the restoration of new creation will be accessible to all. We are the sourdough starter of new creation. Without us, creation will not rise.

Have you ever ridden a bike? Used an iPhone? Texted a friend? Sent a care package? Peeled a potato? Then you've used assistive technology. When we hear the phrase "assistive technology,"

6. Ada María Isasi-Díaz, "Kin-dom of God: A Mujerista Proposal," in *In Our Own Voices: Latino/a Renditions of Theology*, ed. Benjamin Valentin (Maryknoll, NY: Orbis Books, 2010), 171–90.

most of us imagine electric wheelchairs, cochlear implants, and carbon fiber prosthetics, but the history of assistive technology features products that most nondisabled people use every day.

The wheelchair was a precursor to the bike. Stephan Farffler, a paraplegic watchmaker, designed a self-propelled wheelchair in 1655. His hand-controlled three-wheeler led to our modern bicycles and tricycles. His model resembles a recumbent tricycle like the ones you'll find at any beach. The typewriter was invented for a blind woman, Countess Carolina Fantoni da Fivizzano, to write to her lover, Pellegrino Turri, without the use of a scribe. Like WhatsApp, but for the 1800s. In 1874, Alexander Graham Bell worked on a phonautograph to allow d/Deaf students to see vibrations of sound, leading to his work on the telephone. Ring, ring, it's disability justice calling.

Scanners at the post office come from RCA Laboratories' 1949 development of OCR (optical character recognition), which L. E. Flory and W. S. Pike initially designed to read text aloud to blind people. Now OCR is used in scanners, computers, and smartphones all over the world. If you've ever converted a PDF into a Word document, you've used OCR technology. Text messaging was originally designed for people who are d/Deaf. Now millennial culture is texting someone "sorry, can't talk right now" instead of picking up the phone when they call. Entire friendships and family group chats exist over this medium. Texting has become so ubiquitous that it's worrying (read: annoying) when someone calls you. "Is everything OK?" you awkwardly inquire, surprised at the sound of your own voice.

OXO potato peelers. Electronic toothbrushes. Weighted blankets. Twist jar openers. Fidget spinners. Pencil grips. The Snuggie. Audiobooks. Closed-captioning. Touch-screen interfaces. That's right, every time you touch that iPhone, you are using assistive technology. All of these devices were created for and with disabled people. They only became mainstream once folks realized the products could benefit everyone. Living with a disability encourages innovation, because our body-minds do not belong in the current world. Disability is a creative force that allows us to imagine a new world.

This is what the remnant is like. If you design the world with and for disabled people, the entire world benefits. Designing for disabled people to thrive relies on innovative strategies because our body-minds do not fit the norm. Without disabled people's lived experience demonstrating the need for touch screens and potato peelers, the rest of humanity wouldn't benefit. Design for disabled people. The world will follow.

This is what new creation is like. God is making all things new. We are not replaced with a new and improved human model and left in a dump somewhere like discarded Android scraps in an apocalypse. We are not rebooted with our memories wiped until we get it right. (Looking at you, *The Good Place*.) God restores what is already here, with the lame as remnant.

The gist I get from most folks is that disabled people get the leftovers, the crumbs, the hand-me-downs. We might be considered an afterthought, once everyone else is cared for, *if* there is enough money left in the budget. But the history of assistive technology design tells a different story that demands that we revise this exclusory tale. One that shows that your flourishing is tied up in my flourishing. When we are too focused on universal design for the mainstream, we are not as innovative. We don't even realize that we are missing touch screens and texting because no nondisabled person has thought to need them before.

Enter disabled bodies. Our needs are not special. They are human, and you can benefit from the technology designed to meet our very human needs. You probably already have! Let's stop using excuses that disabled people are not worth the cost of inclusion. Apple's profits on the iPhone would beg to differ. Let's stop blaming lack of design on the fact that there are fewer disabled people than nondisabled people. When we thrive, everybody thrives. Next time you send a text, ride a bike, peel a potato, or use a touch screen, remember that it is only possible because a disabled person needed assistive technology and helped innovate an inclusive design. Imagine what we could create if we listened to the needs of disabled people and began rebuilding and reinventing our world. The beautiful thing about the word "building" is that it is both a noun and a verb. We can rebuild what has been here by following the lead of disabled people in our communities. We can reimagine how we might build a new world on the disabled remnant. Imagine what we can create together when we do.

Have you ever watched a TV show or movie for a second time and been surprised by a glaring flaw you never noticed before? (I don't mean wondering why forgettable fop Mark Brendanawicz made it into so many episodes of *Parks and Rec*.) I mean a misplaced ice-cream maker in a galaxy far, far away. In a now-iconic scene in *The Empire Strikes Back*, Willrow Hood frantically flees Galactic Empire invasion, passing Lando and Leia in a Cloud City corridor carrying . . . a Hamilton Beach ice-cream maker? Not even the Force can explain this flaw.

This random background extra's dessert dash is meant to convey a sense of urgency and chaos. The Empire has taken control of the city! Scram! His desperate attempt to save his ice cream at all costs has developed a cult following, an action figure, and a retrofitted backstory via *The Mandalorian*. There's now even a "Running of the Hoods" where fans race, decked out in orange jumpsuits, holding *the* Hamilton Beach 4 Quart Ice Cream Maker. Google it. It's a delight.

Chances are you don't even remember Willrow Hood a.k.a. Ice Cream Maker Guy's run of fame. It's less than two seconds of film time. But once you notice it, you can't *un*notice it. Props are made on a shoestring budget. Meaningless mistakes slip through editing. No film is flawless. Continuity gaffes and Easter eggs are fun to discover when rewatching our favorite movies. They reveal how we are unable to fully take in all the details around us. We must watch and rewatch to receive the entire film. No one can take it all in at once.

Star Wars fanatics love the film—flaws and all—enough to create a community mythos out of this unexplained character who flashes on screen for two seconds. What are the odds that this haphazard ice-cream maker was premeditated? Or that it means anything aside from a background extra's cheap prop? As Han Solo would say, "Never tell me the odds!" The beautiful thing about the *Star Wars* community is that they don't really seem to care whether this is a flaw. They have embraced Willrow and his ice-cream maker regardless of his initial purpose.

Church, we need to be more like *Star Wars* fans. Yes, you read that right. Not everyone is aware of disability inclusion right away, but now that you know, you should embrace crip space in every way possible. Create events around us. Celebrate our eclectic nature. Rejoice alongside us. Stop worrying about the origin of our role or our bodies and instead embrace us as one of your own, ice-cream maker and all.

REFLECTION AND RESPONSE

▶ *Kintsugi* is the Japanese art of restoring broken pottery with gold to create a restored piece.[7] Consider doing this with a group, using broken flatware and repairing items with gold mica powder or liquid gold leaf. This is not a practice of

7. To learn more about *kintsugi*, check out Julie Polter, "The Art of Redeeming Our Battered Era: Artist Makoto Fujimura on Loving What Is Broken and the Holy Work of Repair," *Sojourners*, February 2021, https://sojo.net/magazine/february-2021/art-redeeming-our-battered-era.

fixing but of restoring what was broken. How might this practice of redeeming what was broken give you an embodied understanding of new creation? How can this practice give us an example of the work of restoration that God is bringing about by making the lame a remnant?

▶ If cost were not a factor, how would you reimagine your environment to allow for more inclusion and accessibility? How can you be creative to implement these features in whatever space you are in? In what ways can assistive technology and *Star Wars* model how to consider disabled people as the remnant to build with and around?

▶ Recruit disabled people in your community to regularly lead. Whether it's a Scripture reading, a musical performance, an art project, a silent prayer practice, or a sermon, regularly ask disabled people to lead. Invite the Spirit to work through the holy disruption and prophetic witness of disabled people.

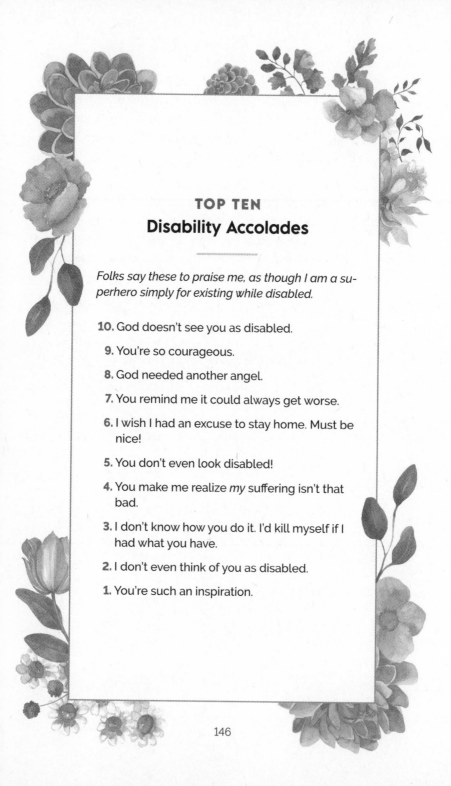

TOP TEN
Disability Accolades

Folks say these to praise me, as though I am a superhero simply for existing while disabled.

10. God doesn't see you as disabled.

9. You're so courageous.

8. God needed another angel.

7. You remind me it could always get worse.

6. I wish I had an excuse to stay home. Must be nice!

5. You don't even look disabled!

4. You make me realize *my* suffering isn't that bad.

3. I don't know how you do it. I'd kill myself if I had what you have.

2. I don't even think of you as disabled.

1. You're such an inspiration.

Disabled God

The woman next to me is crying. Not a few glistening tears elegantly streaming down her cheeks, but the type of sobbing that leaves you panting for shallow breaths. The man across the aisle is jumping up and down as if he's about to go a few rounds in a boxing ring despite his ripped skinny jeans. No one dares to make eye contact with me, but everyone in the congregation glances my way, making sure I hear the promises the lyrics hold for me.

We are at the part of the song that exclaims there'll be "no lame" in heaven because in Jesus's presence we'll finally be "healed and whole." Nondisabled folks couldn't be happier. It's a sea of buffalo plaid arms raised high in the air as the scattered beams of moving lights trace paths through the floating haze. Never mind that I don't feel broken or incomplete. Everyone else is too wrapped up in my erasure to notice.

"Do you realize that Jesus's body will be the only one that isn't perfect in heaven?" the preacher starts. I'm not sure what qualifies him to make such a proclamation. Has he been to heaven? What Bible is he reading? What is a "perfect" body anyway? But no one else seems to question it. In fact, most folks in the crimson-backed pews fervently cheer at this claim, as though someone just announced we're each going home with a brand-new Mercedes. Instead of Oprah shouting "You get a car!" it's a preacher screeching, "You get a perfect body, and *you* get a perfect body, and *you* get a perfect body" to each of us in turn. As if the lack of "perfect" bodies is the predominant thing wrong with our current world.

I'd be more excited that no one hungers or thirsts in new creation, especially since, in our wealthy nation, one in six children don't know where their next meal will come from.[1] But I guess my disabled body would be the focus of your praise if you were just trying to distract yourself from doing something about poverty. Imagining paradise without my wheelchair persuades us that heaven is so far out of reach, such a distant land of miracles where unicorns puke rainbows, that we can't get there no matter how hard we try. Never mind that we have enough food to prevent people from dying of hunger. We just don't want to share it.

People who like to comfort themselves with the idea that disability does not exist in new creation are centering their ableist discomfort in someone else's story—in my story. My disability is not for others to write. My body is not an empty canvas on which nondisabled people can paint their fantasies of new creation. Even if our bodies are not disabled in new creation, why does that make someone so thrilled? When we worship God, we shouldn't harm people who bear God's image. Surely, we can find something to praise about the Creator of the universe that doesn't erase disabled people. Worship should not create a hierarchy of who is in and who is out. Worship should not laud a utopia without your disabled neighbor.

Fantasies of breeding out disability aside, I'm not sure that this preacher's messaging is true. One thing the preacher gets

1. "Facts about Child Hunger in America," Feeding America, 2017, https://www.feedingamerica.org/hunger-in-america/child-hunger-facts.

right: Jesus retained the scars of crucifixion. But who's to say we will be any different?

When Daniel visits the clouds of heaven, he describes how the "throne was fiery flames, and its wheels were burning fire" (Dan. 7:9). A chair with wheels sounds a lot like a wheelchair to me, and one that gives new meaning to burning rubber. Maybe that's something we should sing about. Cue the swelling acoustic guitar music.

Conveniently, the animated chorus forgets that God's throne is a fiery wheelchair when they buzz about heaven. I'm told this is a metaphor, not to take things so literally. But if anyone bothered to ask me, they would know that when I picture an idyllic world, I picture ramps. How else would my upgraded flaming wheelchair get around?

Driving home from the service, I reconsider these assumptions that seemingly impacted no one else but me. The palm fronds pass by in a blur as I wonder to myself, not for the first time, what churches would be like if pastors understood God in the way that I do: as disabled. What if everything we think about bodies—every idea that some bodies are better than others—is wrong? What if everything we've imagined about new creation is built on these limited assumptions? What if we could imagine mobility devices as similar to the one God uses to reign?

Turns out it's not just me and Daniel. Ezekiel describes God with a massive mobility device that is lifted by four angels with fused legs and colossal wheels. The wheels encase wheels that glisten like topaz (Ezek. 1:15–21). God uses a fiery, shimmering, turquoise wheelchair to get around, and so should I.[2]

I am certainly not the first person to think of God as disabled. Nancy Eiesland, who pioneered disability theology, imagined

---

2. I am not attempting to exegete the text here or arguing that this is the author's intent. I am showing one way that God has met me through this passage. I am not building a doctrine on this. I am meeting with the God who sees.

God in a sip-and-puff wheelchair. After a friend declared that her disability would be removed in heaven, Eiesland was horrified because she felt that would erase a part of who she was and how she understood God.[3] To nondisabled people, this is particularly difficult to understand because of the hypothesis that disability is always bad or a result of the fall, something to be redeemed *from* in the new creation. To imagine God as disabled seems to diminish God's power or presence. "God can't be disabled," they inform me. "That's insulting to the heart of the Creator of the universe," another retorts. What's insulting to God is when we don't consider disabled people image-bearers. Or when we can only imagine paradise by erasing one-quarter of humanity. Or when we don't feed the least of these when it is well within our power to do so.

I am not interested in adding to the will-we-or-won't-we-be-disabled-in-heaven conversation. On some level, it doesn't matter if our heavenly bodies will be disabled or not. No one can know that. It is out of my control and does nothing to restore the way I am treated now. But at the very least, I would like to be able to go to church without listening to folks impose their unexamined theology on me. Without being bombarded with so many "somedays" and "at leasts" and "you'll be running/kick-boxing/flying/fixed/whole/human in heaven." How we think about eschatology influences how we treat people today. We can't simply put eschatology in another box in our brains. If we believe that disabled people are not whole until they cross an enchanted threshold into the afterlife, that will certainly impact the way we engage with them in the here and now. We talk about God's kingdom as the now and not yet: the in-between space that we get glimpses of but are not fully a part of yet. Treating disabled people as image-bearers only once we get to the not yet

3. Nancy Eiesland, *The Disabled God: Toward a Liberatory Theology of Disability* (Nashville: Abingdon, 1994), 174–76.

impacts the now. Let disabled people lead in imagining what new creation could be for us. For some, that's using wheelchairs; for others, it is not. For some, it includes God using ASL. For others, it means seeing. Who's to say it will be the same for all of us? The disability community is a diverse group of various physicalities, mentalities, and beliefs. Learn from us when we tell you how we imagine restoration. Let our imaginations for restoration light the way.

There are those who will counter that I am a beloved child of God, so it doesn't matter what my body looks like or how it functions. This one is well-intentioned, but it fails to understand a key aspect of my identity. I am disabled. I don't say that to garner pity or to overemphasize my disability. I fully recognize that it is not the totality of my identity either. But the truth is, being disabled is a core part of the way I interact with the world and with God. Kind acquaintances often want to justify erasing disability by claiming that it just doesn't matter. "God doesn't see you as disabled," they promise. Why should it matter if we celebrate that there are no more disabled people in heaven, when your core identity is in Christ? Here's why it matters. Imagine if folks cheered for a song that touted "no more brown eyes in heaven." That's a quality that you didn't choose and you can't change. Perhaps some days you don't even *like* your brown eyes. None of us can know if our eye color will endure in a new-creation reality. But a whole crowd chanting, cheering, and celebrating that your eyes won't be brown might feel a bit squidgy. Imagine how you might feel with them belting out, "No more brown-eyed girls, because we'll finally be healed and whole." Guess God isn't a fan of Van Morrison.

Folks who want to erase my disability in the name of embracing how God understands me are still erasing my disability. The idea that our bodies don't matter to God is a lovely idea that comes from a warm place with a cozy blanket, but it is not true. To be sure, I am a beloved child of God, but it *does* matter what happens to my body. Our bodies matter. If they didn't, why would Jesus bother with the incarnation? Seems messy to go through all that spit and sweat and suffering if it was *merely* about souls. Jesus could have snapped a finger, Thanos-style, and waved goodbye to the dominions of darkness. It certainly would have been so much cleaner (and less painful) that way.

But Jesus chose to take on a body and enter what it means to be human, even all the snotty bits we blush about. The Word became flesh, and we try to turn it back into words again. Our theology is incarnational because bodies matter. To say that it doesn't matter if I am disabled is to dismiss the incarnation. Maybe if we started acknowledging that, we wouldn't treat prayer like a genie granting wishes. Maybe then we could acknowledge someone else's pain without quickly changing the subject. Maybe then we could stop blaming disabled bodies on the fall. Maybe then we would understand that all of us—disabled and nondisabled people—are made in the image of God.

It isn't about whether disabilities exist in new creation. They exist now. If you can't imagine a restored world without getting rid of 25 percent of the people in this country and 15 percent of people globally, there is something askew with the imagination. It is simply too small for our big God. Whether we have brown eyes or wheelchairs in new creation, we shouldn't celebrate the erasure of those traits here and now. Most people don't even realize they are doing this. They have conflated disability with suffering and assume it's best to erase both. The issue is, not all disabled people suffer from their disabilities. Not all disabled people want those disabilities changed. But *all* of us suffer from ableist assumptions about people's bodies. All of us suffer from limited imaginations that confine God's creation to replicating Barbie doll versions of humanity.

What if wheelchairs became like glasses? Glasses are correctives, to be sure. We know they act as ocular prosthetics to assist folks to see more crisply. Yet I have never learned of anyone with glasses targeted for curative prayers or shaming calls to repentance. Glasses are a fashion statement, so specifically tailored to someone's aesthetic that some don specs just to look geek chic. Cat eye, aviator, shield, rimless, tortoiseshell; the shapes and styles are boundless. What if we did the same for mobility devices? Instead of stigmatizing wheelchairs, scooters, and canes, what if we celebrated them as fashion statements for disabled folks?

Mobility devices should be functional and effective, but that has never prevented us from designing beautiful, quirky glasses. My cane is royal blue, but what if it were molded to look like Wonder Woman's magical sword? Seriously, can someone make this for me? What if my scooter had fiery images inside the wheels to create a flip-book effect when I'm zipping down the pavement?

My wheels liberate me and allow me to operate in tandem with my scooter, Diana. Her tires grip the pavement, absorbing the shock waves that my legs would otherwise have to endure. I lean into her slightly as we curve around a corner, like water gently caressing the riverbank as it flows. I feel the texture of the earth, the rhythm of the cement. I hear the symphony of vibrations as we drift from concrete to cobblestone. My physicality does not stop at the tip of my toes or the crown of my head; it extends to the frame of my cobalt chair, able to transport me to new worlds. Just as in Ezekiel's vision, I am fused with these wheels that are my ticket to freedom. I am body, wheels, and fire.

If only people could imagine my wheels in the way they do glasses. My nieces and nephew certainly do. To their vibrant minds, my scooter makes me cool. They don't interpret anything about my mobility devices as tragic, which shows the impact of the kill-or-cure narratives we construct around disability. They think it's exciting that I get to zip around. Perhaps if we recovered this childlike faith of witnessing the beauty in all bodies, we could sing about new creation in a way that included all of us. I do not know if I will be disabled in new creation, but I know there won't be pain, and it's painful for people to celebrate erasing part of me. Maybe what needs healing isn't my body, but society. Maybe people will come to appreciate that disability is not a sad form but a cultural identity with its own wealth of lessons, just like my nephew and nieces do.

Maybe what will be healed is ableism.

So many of us have been taught to understand disability from a loss model. We believe that disabled bodies have lost the ability to do something: to walk, to run, to speak, to ride a bike. I understand that to many nondisabled folks, I cannot walk "normally." That is true, but it's not the whole story. It negates the fact that I can *glide*. Wheelchairs are freedom, many of my fellow wheelchair users say. They allow us to move freely throughout the world. When I use my wheels, folks who are walking must keep up with me. I ride off into the sunset before they ever realize where I've skyrocketed. What if we recognized disability as a necessary disruption to the status quo? What if we understood disability not through potential loss, but through its multitude of gains? If we allowed more room for biodiversity, we might come to fully embrace disabled people as bringing their own cultural narrative and embodied wisdom to our communities. We might even embrace our disabled God.

Somehow folks are more comfortable with God as an inanimate object or an animal than they are with God as disabled. In Scripture, God is variously imagined as a mother hen (Luke 13:34), a bear robbed of her cubs (Hosea 13:8), an eagle hovering over her nest (Deut. 32:11–12), a lamb (Rev. 19:7), a rock, fortress, and deliverer (Ps. 18:2), a potter (Isa. 64:8), a woman in labor (Isa. 42:14), and a comforting mother (Isa. 66:13).

These are metaphors to help us understand one aspect of the vast mystery that is God. Yet it is illuminating that most people are more comfortable singing songs to rocks than they are with the idea that God might be disabled.

Crooked, the white coats say. My leg is crooked. My alignment is off. But little in nature is straight; creation is jagged—the bumpy trunks of redwoods, the snaking branches of elm trees, the ragged edges of maple leaves—nature is delightfully crooked. It is human-made stuff that is straight, orderly, and logical. But God's canvas of creation is wild, unruly, and exquisitely messy. Or, to put it the way Paul does, God's "invisible qualities" are "clearly seen" throughout the "creation of the world" (Rom. 1:20 NIV). Creation—in all its gunk and grit—displays the "eternal power and divine nature" of God to us. And it is delightfully crooked.

Consider the penguin. Our tuxedo-wearing friends waddle, feet turned outward, shuffling side to side. It's easy to think their gait is clunky, silly—even when compared to the human's vertical stride. Penguins' short steps trundle their stubby legs forward incrementally. Yet their walk is far more efficient than the human gait. Penguins have the highest energy recovery rate of any terrestrial animal. This simply means they retain their energy moving from one stride to the next.[4] Humans fall forward with each step, allowing gravity to sludge our bodies along. But the ever-efficient penguins rock from side to side in a way that preserves their energy for much longer. What's more, the safest way to move on ice is to emulate the penguin, because it increases stability on slippery surfaces by lowering the center of gravity. Turns out we should all do the penguin shuffle when traversing icy terrain. No tuxedo required.

What if when we pictured the penguin, we didn't think of a funky shuffle, but a safer, more resourceful way to move? Instead

4. Kate Wong, "Why Penguins Waddle," *Scientific American*, December 21, 2020, https://www.scientificamerican.com/article/why-penguins-waddle.

of mocking these dapper birds, we should learn from them. We should consider the ways an irregular gait might improve our lives. We should invite disability to teach us something instead of assuming nondisabled bodies are perfect and complete. We don't experience the remainder of nature in this way. It is only for human bodies that we have developed a hierarchy of worth. No one claims the calla lily's limp petals have petal deficit syndrome. Or that lions have chronic fatigue for lounging all day. The emu is not weaker than the sparrow because it cannot fly. We do not look down on the octopus because it is deaf, or moles or cave fish because they are blind. In this way, disability becomes a conceptual category, a methodology, a way of interpreting the world through biodiversity. Disability is more than wheelchairs and braille. It's a way of understanding the world by disrupting categories of normalcy. It's a way of discovering the beautiful biodiversity that God has woven throughout the tapestry of creation.

If we thought of disability in this way, it wouldn't bother us that God is described as disabled throughout Scripture. God is portrayed as d/Deaf in many of the psalms. Frustrated by God's lack of audible response, the psalmists often cast God as one who cannot—or will not—hear their pleas of anguish. Why is this so bad? Many d/Deaf people characterize their abilities not as "hearing loss" but "Deaf gain."[5] Perhaps if we learned to heed instead of simply hearing, we would realize the diverse ways that God communicates with us. Maybe God uses Deaf gain to develop *us*. Silence is the space for God to listen to us, for us to be still and sit with the mystery and muck of our lives. Maybe a lack of God speaking in ways we anticipate develops a deep listening in us and gives us space to figure ourselves out.

5. Of course, many d/Deaf people do consider themselves to be disabled. For more information, check out Danny Ko, "D/deafness," in *Skin, Tooth, and Bone: The Basis of Our Movement Is Our People; A Disability Justice Primer*, by Sins Invalid, 2nd ed. (Berkeley: Sins Invalid, 2019), 88–93.

Deaf gain is that God's supposed silence can be revelatory, help us process, and develop us.

In Romans, Paul describes the way the Spirit communicates, assuring us that when we don't know what to pray, the Spirit "intercedes for us through wordless groans" (Rom. 8:26 NIV). These groanings too deep to utter call to mind the communication experience of some folks with intellectual or developmental disabilities. Mute, nonverbal, dumb, or silent, they are harshly labeled. Usually, it's the rest of us who are not paying attention to their wordless groans or diverse range of communication styles. Society dismisses their cadence as irregular because it cannot form an imagination for how to communicate outside structured, alphabetic text. Yet the Spirit interacts using groans and unintelligible language that cannot be contained by our formulaic systems.

Grunts, groans, and sighs borrow the language of the Spirit, where every breath becomes the word of the living God. The language of the soul needn't be verbalized in words. All it takes is the melody of a Queen song to give you all the feels. Sometimes you even find yourself singing the music, not just the lyrics. Words are just the frosting on top of the emotional cake. Frosting can be delicious, but too much of it sends the stomach spinning. Perhaps if we listened to the groans, we might come to understand the Spirit's messages. Perhaps if we developed the patience and practice of attending to diverse communication styles, we could learn from those with intellectual and developmental disabilities in our communities.

God is not just d/Deaf or "nonverbal," but sometimes blind in Scripture. In Psalm 139, David wonders at the fact that "even the darkness is not dark to you; the night is as bright as the day, for darkness is as light to you" (Ps. 139:12). When read from a disability-theology perspective, this psalm takes on new meaning about how light and darkness are indistinguishable to God, who is not confined to the sensory experiences that guide many of our sighted interactions. Some people who are blind report a similar phenomenon, where light and darkness are perceived as analogous to each other.[6] Darkness is no longer weighed down by fear and dread; it becomes a neutral state of being. In this way, people who are blind or low vision might experience an aspect of God's constancy that those of us with sight do not.

These are just a few examples of how shifting to a disability-gains model can help broaden our understanding of God. Instead of conflating blindness with ignorance, we could learn from the way it displays the steadfastness of God. Instead of dismissing people who are "nonverbal" as unintelligent, we could learn from their groans too deep to utter. Instead of pitying d/Deaf folks for hearing loss, we could learn from the revelatory space of Deaf gain. Instead of mocking wheelchairs, we could perceive them as resplendent as God's fiery throne. We should learn from a variety of disabled perspectives and the unique cultural wealth that they can share with the body of Christ. I can't write about the experience of being d/Deaf or blind any more than a nondisabled person can write about using a wheelchair. Disability is a broad constellation of experience, and I don't represent the entire community. I am just one disabled girl, sitting in front of the church, asking them to love us. We need to learn from the embodied experiences of people with different types of disabilities to deepen our understanding of God, Scripture, and an embodied life of faith. The more that we expand our understanding of human experience, the more that we can learn about one another and imagine how each disability illustrates God to the world. We are all made in God's image, after all. Imagine the possibilities if we experienced bodily difference not as defect or loss but as a unique opportunity to experience

6. John M. Hull, *In the Beginning There Was Darkness* (Harrisburg, PA: Trinity Press International, 2002), 159–60.

the diversity of a vast creator God. It just might make the body of Christ healed and whole.

Tick, tock.

"Did the doctor tell you how long?" she wonders earnestly, trying to gauge how serious my condition is. Her shoulders shrink when I tell her it's anybody's guess. It's not like I can mark my calendar with an ambulatory due date.

Tick, tock, tock.

Wet, dense sand cakes onto my numb toes as I shuffle without knowing whether my legs will catch me. Soft hues of purple and pink bruise the sky over the undulating water. I push past the piercing fire in my ankle in the name of desensitization training, the breeze whispering the scent of salt and sunscreen. I fall, I rise, I fall again, the sand supposedly training my body to counteract the muscle atrophy. I watch the grains graze my inner ankle and tell myself it is fine, even though it feels like fire. I log the time spent pushing myself, not knowing whether it will be wasted.

Tock, tick, tock.

The physical therapist's enthusiasm pulses through the clinic. I try not to focus on her gritted teeth, which barely veil her honeyed anticipation that today will be the day I stand without my cane, because it will soon sour to dismay if I cannot. My arms propel me, but my body slumps back down in the chair before I can shift all my weight to my left side. Another therapist's face is the mirror image of my ornery body, melting with disappointment like mint chip in August.

Tock, tick, tick, tock.

It is time to call it. I had scheduled to go to hot pot with friends, but my body made other plans. By the sun, it is 5:30 p.m.; by my body, it is time-out. More plans undone by the stroke of crip time. "Out of spoons; have fun without me," I text my friends. Ba-doop—the familiar text tone travels through the airwaves between us. "Let's do it when you have the spoons," the blue bubble on my phone reads. Warmed and worn out, I climb into bed, unable to do anything else.

Tick, tock, tick.

Pungent chlorine overpowers the muggy air. Each pace is weighed down by the force of the warm water against my delicate limbs. Buoyancy a distant dream, I fight the torrent to get to the other side, to combat my muscle atrophy. Everyone else in the pool is old enough to be my grandparent. They gape at me, their wrinkled stares revealing their curiosity at me—a millennial—in aquatic physical therapy. They reassure me that they know how it feels for a body to "slow down." Externally smiling, inwardly cringing, I don't have the energy to tell them that slowing down at seventy is not the same thing as at eleven. My adolescence was never fast.

Tock, tick, tick.

Jolt. I wake with a jolt. Pain surges through my body like a fire alarm. "Wake up!" it commands. The darkness is enveloping, cast aside only by the blue light emanating from my phone. I check the time: 2:36, it reads. I breathe, meditate, and pray, but the spasms overpower any dream of sleep, until I finally decide to just accept that I am awake. Sludging to the kettle, I tell myself to honor what my body tells me instead of forcing it to speak clock.

Tick, tock, tock, tock.

"*When* will you feel better?" a sympathetic stranger probes at the public library, ogling my scooter a little too close for comfort. I am so exhausted that I overshare details he isn't asking about in hopes of showing how intrusive this question is from a stranger. Somehow, tampons still possess scare power. There is no *when*. My body operates on crip time.

Tock, tock, tock.

Crip time. The idea that time does not progress in a linear way that would allow disabled people to experience a predictable future with planned outcomes. Disability disrupts normative notions of time found in clocks and calendars. It unsettles the assumed life span and activities attached to any given life stage. Past, present, and potential future are incoherent, jumbled like a drawer of power cords you can't disentangle. Even the concept of prognosis assumes a future time, a state when you are no longer ill, as if disability comes with an expiration date like a carton of milk.

Grief is the way that most of us familiarize ourselves with this fluidity of time. You're fine. Then one Tuesday at work, you catch the whiff of your grandma's soap, and you are transported to the day she died. You become a living monument to the memory of her, your grief a comfort in preserving the only scented fragment left of her.

Crip time functions in a similar way. I am a living prognosis. Instead of forcing my body to adhere to the clock, crip time "bends the clock to fit the demands of the disabled body and mind."[7] I am a melting clock in a Salvador Dalí. Time explodes into a million shattered pieces of bodily experience, like glass shards crunching underfoot. There is no projected development for my body. The future itself is precarious. I exist in the liminal temporality of crip time.

But then again, so might God. Isaiah tells us that God "inhabits eternity" (Isa. 57:15). The psalmist writes, "For a thousand years in your sight are like yesterday when it is past, or like a watch in the night" (Ps. 90:4). Peter echoes this idea: "With the Lord one day is like a thousand years, and a thousand years are like one day" (2 Pet. 3:8). God is omnipresent and everlasting, situated outside the linear confines of our clocks. The way God

7. Ellen Samuels, "Six Ways of Looking at Crip Time," *Disability Studies* 37, no. 3 (2017), https://dsq-sds.org/article/view/5824/4684.

inhabits time, unfolded, cyclical, and nonlinear, can be understood through the experience of crip time and the disabled body.

My body moves backward in time. My body has brought my left leg back to life more times than I can count. I don't mean this in a churchy way, the way we might pray for God to "irrigate the deserts of our souls" or "resurrect" our faith while everyone dramatically *mm-hmm*s. I mean that I know what it's like to look down and see a withered limb where muscle "should" be. I know the sensation of willing my ligaments to tap to a beat while my ankle stubbornly remains stationary; for my left leg to be twenty degrees colder than my right. I know what it's like for my limb to be blue and bald from lack of circulation, for doctors to whisper the word "amputation" with eyes glued to the floor.

I have witnessed my scrawny, frigid, sapphire leg transform from bone to muscle and back to bone. Even the miracle of shaving my legs was once unattainable to me, and likely it will be again. My body is an ever-ticking clock, yet it doesn't always move forward or even move consistently. It reverses, speeds up, and works in slow motion. To some, this might seem scary or strange, but to us, it is liberating. We are not confined to the rigid clock, only able to advance incrementally before resetting again tomorrow. We move freely and fluidly. Disability helps us understand God in a different capacity because we know what it means to shift backward and forward in time with no justification for our progress or regression. We know how we have worth and value even when the minutes and hours and years pass without us "accomplishing" anything. We know because we've had to learn a life outside time.

Imagine if our work schedules, parenting duties, or social calendars were shaped around our unique needs and daily ability, not by cultural imperatives and economic demands. Longevity. We desire longevity in life, relationships, and careers. We celebrate someone who retires after decades on the job; we are in awe of couples who celebrate their fiftieth anniversary. Yet we do next to nothing to make our lives sustainable, beyond collective praise and individual prowess. We create punishing schedules within demanding systems that show little concern for our well-being. We kill ourselves to speak clock. Our mode of living is fast-paced, instant-gratification workaholism.

Those of us who are disabled cannot keep up. No amount of pushing myself harder has changed the fact that I am disabled (and believe me, high school me certainly tried). I live by spoons, not clocks. Crip time has given me a richer understanding of God's relationship to time. I imagine God as everlasting but temporal. God is with us in our particular moment in time, while not being confined by its limits. Psalm 90:2 tells us, "Before the mountains were brought forth, or ever you had formed the earth and the world, from everlasting to everlasting you are God." God exists before Abraham, before the mountains were formed, and is still with us now. God predates the very notion of time.

We don't really know how God experiences time. Is God timeless or temporal? Does God engage with time as in *Arrival* (where backward causation and emotions influence a cyclical experience of time), *Back to the Future* (where a single timeline can be rewritten as time progresses), or *Watchmen* (where Doctor Manhattan is aware of the future via a time loop and carries it out, regardless of the personal consequences)? Or somehow all three? We may never know. Philosophers and theologians, whether they be on "Team Timeless" or "Team Temporal" (or even the mediators, "Team Timeless, then Temporal"), all seem to agree that God's experience of time is different from the linear, unidirectional stream most of us humans set our watches to.

We'll likely never fully comprehend God's experience of (with?) time, but we do know that crip time allows us one way to understand nonlinear time. Some days I need help putting on my shoes. My tentative toes tip across the fiery bed of nails felt by my body. The pain rolls through my calf and up my hip, like billows of steam when getting out of the shower. Twitch. My nerves contort my toes against my will. My ankle is stone. Menthol and cinnamon ointments assault my nostrils. I trudge like one pulled down by sopping jeans against the tide. The next day, I prance more nimbly. There is no rationale or reason to crip time.

It used to bother me. I wanted my life to fit neatly into a day planner, with different color codes for each type of event. Blue for work, red for doctors, green for fun, naturally. But after attempting to organize every activity into neat, contained, color-coded slots, I realized that my body doesn't play by the rules of Filofax. My life became a series of canceled plans and disappointing withdrawals.

Living with crip time has allowed me to experience the fullness of God in a different way. I don't develop on the same schedule as nondisabled people. I can't plan how my body will be tomorrow. Crip time makes me dependent on something other than myself. It forces me to be present. All plans are in pencil. Time slows down to meet me where I am. Other moments, it speeds up, as though I am already eighty-five years old, ready for dinner at 4 p.m., followed by bed. There is no pattern to the way my body experiences time. Believe me, I have tracked its peaks and valleys at various points in my life, and no rhythm emerges. The only thing that's consistent is its inconsistency— each day a mystery for how much time it contains.

Whenever I get frustrated by my lack of scheduled time, I remind myself that Jesus never seems to be in a hurry. Perhaps Jesus operates via crip time just like me. Instead of rushing to the next thing or trying to keep up, Jesus slows down to meet us where we are. Not motivated by FOMO or appointments, Jesus's patient pace invites people to journey alongside him at the speed of love. It is slow and sporadic, but it is worth it. The three-mile-an-hour God operates at the speed of love.[8] God's time leaves space for

8. Kosuke Koyama, *Three Mile an Hour God* (Maryknoll, NY: Orbis Books, 1980). For more on time and dementia, check out John Swinton, *Becoming Friends of Time* (Waco: Baylor University Press, 2018).

wandering, withering, and waddling. It reminds us that love is older than time. Love cannot be contained by clocks.

Crip time develops a deeper presence in us. It invites us to value ourselves outside of productivity and capitalism. It claims that life is cherished regardless of how it is lived or what it achieves. It declares that each day matters. Not because of how much you get checked off the to-do list, but because you are present to the presence of the living God. It develops a muscle memory for endurance beyond the markers of success. It allows us to be present with one another without expectations or future goals. In the face of the lie, it declares the truth: that every body-mind radiates God's timeless image to the world, and that is enough. We are enough.

Regardless of whether you are disabled, you can experience crip time alongside us. You don't need to function according to a list of "shoulds" predetermined before your life began. By age eighteen, you'll graduate. Wedding bells by thirty-five. Before forty, you'll own a house—nay, a shiny mansion—with room for your 2.5 kids. Says who? There is no "on time" or "on track" when it comes to a life of faith. There is no road map for wandering in the wilderness. Following the cloud cannot be charted. It's about time we stopped forcing our bodies to speak clock. You can embrace the experience of crip time that is fluid and cyclical, not worrying about how it is perceived. You don't have to burden yourself with what you have accomplished today but can rest in the truth of your belovedness. Maybe if we all embraced crip time, we could invest time in ensuring our neighbors flourish alongside us instead of constantly being "too busy" to get involved. Maybe then we could transform into something more Christlike. We, too, could move at the speed of love.

I have always loved Good Friday. Easter morning's corporate call and response ("He is risen." "He is risen, *indeed!*") at a service adorned with lilies and everyone in their Sunday best has never been my vibe. The disabled God, on the cross, is the one I most relate to. I'd probably still follow that Jesus even without the resurrection.

Particularly in the Protestant church, we cannot handle Jesus on the cross. We are so focused on the triumphalism of it all, the victory of Easter Sunday and the excitement of going to a bustling brunch and eating Peeps until we need a nap. Dyed eggs everywhere. Why do we hide them, though? Easter celebrations have never made sense to me: Everyone suddenly in agreement that it's appropriate to start the service at sunrise. It's the one day a year that we pretend to like ham.

But Good Friday matters. Jesus's sorrow and death matters, and not to shame us into following the suffering servant. We cannot skip to Easter Sunday without acknowledging the transformative power of the cross. Good Friday is the one day on the liturgical calendar when we revel in what happened on that hill in Golgotha before repressing it the remainder of the year.

Everyone seems so embarrassed by the despair of Good Friday. It's a day when we reflect, repent, and regret the whole killing Jesus thing. "The Nails in Your Hands" bellows a somber tone. Eyes glued to the floor, weight shifting back and forth as they fidget, churchgoers dwell on their own gunk on Good Friday. Admittedly, the collective hatred displayed on Good Friday can be overwhelming. When confronted with our own mess, we focus on the crucifixion out of our convictions about the ways we are steeped in the dominions of darkness. The crucifixion shows how collective humanity rejected Jesus. It displays the worst of us. Every cosmic sin of destruction, domination, and dominion is on prominent display in the crucifixion. It's humiliating. It's grotesque. It's worth feeling the gravity of. Jesus certainly did.

But the cross isn't embarrassing. There is a big difference between the crucifixion—what we did to Jesus—and the cross—what Jesus did for us.[9] The cross is worth *boasting* about. Paul even tells us so in Galatians: "May I never boast of anything except the cross of our Lord Jesus Christ, by which the world has been crucified to me, and I to the world" (Gal. 6:14). Paul isn't boasting about the crucifixion. That would be morbid and weird, even for Paul. He's boasting in the cross: the redemptive power of the suffering servant. The mystery of the cross is how Jesus triumphs in the midst of the destruction of the crucifixion. Various atonement theories have tried to explain how the mysterious event of salvation works, but the power of the cross cannot be fully explained by our limited understanding. We try transactional analogies and legal comparisons to approximate it, but we can't fully grasp the splendor of it all.

We may not fully comprehend how the cross works, but we sense its power. To behold Jesus on the cross is to witness the clearest depiction of a God who is love emptied out for us, taking on the dominions of darkness and suffering under the weight of systemic oppression to reveal God's grace to us all.

When we talk about the idea that death has no sting, we are not simply naysaying morbidity, but affirming the concept that we no longer live in bondage to the fear of death because Jesus defeated it on the cross. Many of us imagine a superhero "POW!" punch when we read words like "defeated" or "triumphed." Jesus showed death—hooray! Grab your superhero gear today. But defeating death happens on the cross. Jesus actively destroys the power of death and sin, nailing it to the cross, and restoring us in the process (Col. 2:13–14). Jesus doesn't need a superhero's cape or dramatic fight scene with punctuated BAMs and KABOOMs to do it. Jesus's power is cruciform. Jesus's power is in disability.[10]

9. For more on this, check out Bradley Jersak, *A More Christlike God: A More Beautiful Gospel* (Pasadena, CA: Plain Truth Ministries, 2016).

10. Martin Albl states, "Paul describes Christ as 'disabled' and 'powerful.' He preached not only 'Christ crucified,' the 'disabled' Christ ('crucified in weakness,' 2 Cor. 13:4), but also the glorified, powerful Christ—the Christ beyond all disabilities, including the

Jesus on the cross is disabled, physically impaired by sweating drops of blood while nailed to a wooden stake. Jesus is also disabled in a social sense. A person who was crucified bore the weight of social stigma in the ancient world, highlighting the social model of disability. Jesus inverts all our shame and preconceived notions about what power looks like into a cross. Jesus disables himself on our behalf. This goes directly against our notions of self-preservation and victory by demonstrating how God's power is self-emptying, radically forgiving, and displayed through disability. The disabled Christ is the definitive revelation of God to humanity. The disabled body is the source of our redemption.

In Christian circles, we often say the way to be Christlike is to take up your cross and follow Jesus. We sing songs about it and put it on water bottle stickers, but we rarely live it. To access God's power, we don't need prosperity prayers or militarized mantras. We need people to take up the cruciform power of emptying out for the sake of the least of these. We need folks to stop hoarding power and pass the mic. We need people to stop stockpiling resources and share with one another. We long for God to come in glory and power in a way that makes sense to us: bringing us wealth, health, and happiness. Basically, we want Jesus to be an Instagram influencer with a picture-perfect life worthy of trending hashtags. But God rarely works in the ways we expect. Instead, God's power looks like a cross. The truest revelation of who God is, the decisive victory over the dominions of darkness, is a disabled Jesus, emptying out for our sake on a dishonorable cross (1 John 4:8; John 14:9; Heb. 1:3).

Jesus shows us how to take up our cross as a daily, ongoing struggle, not a one-time event. All too often, this is weaponized

---

limitation of death itself (Rom. 6:9). It is the paradoxical connection between the two that is the center of Paul's message." Albl, "'For Whenever I Am Weak, Then I Am Strong': Disability in Paul's Epistles," in *This Able Body*, ed. Hector Avalos, Sarah J. Melcher, and Jeremy Schipper (Atlanta: Society of Biblical Literature, 2007), 148.

against marginalized groups to glorify suffering. It does not mean we demand suffering endurance from others. It encourages us to stop hoarding whatever power or privilege we have and to invest in the flourishing of the entire community of creation. Taking up a cross means following Jesus's example of self-emptying, radically forgiving love for the sake of someone else. That is the profound power of our disabled God.

Jesus isn't into the big acts of power that we humans dream up in our revenge fantasies. Boom, "the palace of the Roman governor" explodes while Jesus calmly walks away unscathed (John 18:28 NIV). "Bet your hands are dirty now, Pilate!" you can hear him mutter underneath his breath while holding the singed detonator. The way Jesus defeats the dominions of darkness could have included military might in epic battle scenes with no need of CGI. But Jesus's power is cruciform. It might seem foolish to some, but God doesn't use blasts like a boss from our revenge fantasies; God takes up a cross instead. God still whispers in the still, small voice. God subverts our ideas of what power looks like. And it looks like disability.

I am resigned to live a life of foolishness. I smell like lidocaine patches. Cords dangle from my body. My "never tell me the odds" Millennium Falcon slippers have paced the halls of my workplace, as they are often the only footwear I can manage. I have had to let go of concepts like "professionalism," "productivity," and "independence." My husband often helps me put my clothes *on*, which is a fun reversal that purity culture didn't warn me about.

My body defies age and expectation since it runs on crip time. Perhaps this is what it means to not be ashamed of the gospel, the incarnation, and the cross. I refuse to be ashamed of my disabled body because it displays the crucified Christ. It is twisted and twitchy and tired, but it is triumphant.

Disabled people know what it means for word to take on flesh, because our bodies declare that reality. We are the breathing

169

incarnations of medical diagnoses that doctors spend years studying but still don't understand. We know what it means to lose your life and for the world to scorn our bodies. "Lame, crippled, degenerate," they call me. "You walk like you have a stick up your butt," they shout. We inherit the shame of previous generations who tried to kill us off, only for us to survive. "Better off dead than disabled," they say. "Merciful," they call our murders. We are the face of difference that power rejects.

Ask yourself: Can you behold the truest revelation of who God is on the cross? Can you encounter your disabled neighbors with the same reverence and awe? Next time you approach a disabled person, can you search their face for the disabled Christ?

We are called to share in the suffering and death of Christ by taking up our cross on behalf of others. We are called to share whatever power or privilege we have so everyone can flourish. We are called to be disabled.

REFLECTION AND RESPONSE

▶ Create a piece of art in any medium and style reimagining God as disabled, as discussed in this chapter. How can experiencing the presence of God through art refresh your concept of disability? Post your art to the Disability Justice Hub at MyBodyIsNotAPrayerRequest.com and to social media with the hashtag #DisabledGod and #MyBodyIsNotAPrayerRequest.

Accessibility note: Please make sure to capitalize the beginning of each word in the hashtag and offer an image description to make your post more accessible to people who use screen readers.

▶ Rewrite the lyrics of any worship song or liturgical prayer that dismisses disabled bodies or minds. You don't have to "cancel" the entire song; you can help redeem it by shifting the lines that are not welcoming to our disabled neighbors.

In a song such as "You Hold Me Now" by Hillsong UNITED, the lyric "no sick or lame" could become "no fear or shame."[11] In "Forever Reign" by Hillsong, the line "when my fear is crippling" could become "when my fear is threatening," and the chorus could be changed from "I'm running to your arms" to "I'm rushing to your arms."[12] The famous line from John Newton's "Amazing Grace" could become "was bound, but now I'm free" instead of "was blind, but now I see."[13] These changes are small and easy, but they have a huge impact. If I attended a service where folks made an effort to change ableist language in a song, I would certainly feel welcomed and valued.

11. Matt Crocker and Reuben Morgan, "You Hold Me Now," on *Across the Earth: Tear Down the Walls*, Capitol Christian Music, Hillsong Music, 2009.

12. Reuben Morgan and Jason Ingram, "Forever Reign," on *A Beautiful Exchange*, Hillsong LIVE, 2010.

13. Suggested by Stephanie Tait (@StephTaitWrites), "Amazing Grace. Whenever I sing it, I change the ableist lyrics," Twitter, October 19, 2020, 12:46 p.m., https://twitter.com/StephTaitWrites/status/1318232031898185728.

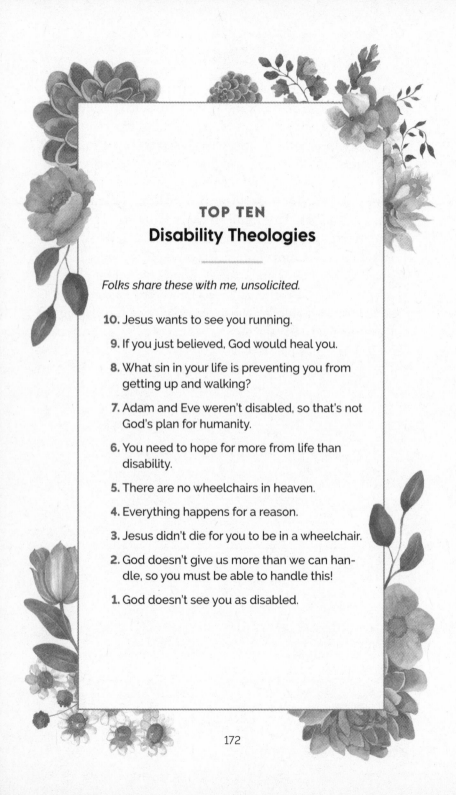

TOP TEN
Disability Theologies

Folks share these with me, unsolicited.

10. Jesus wants to see you running.

9. If you just believed, God would heal you.

8. What sin in your life is preventing you from getting up and walking?

7. Adam and Eve weren't disabled, so that's not God's plan for humanity.

6. You need to hope for more from life than disability.

5. There are no wheelchairs in heaven.

4. Everything happens for a reason.

3. Jesus didn't die for you to be in a wheelchair.

2. God doesn't give us more than we can handle, so you must be able to handle this!

1. God doesn't see you as disabled.

Disabled Church

Where does it end?" he asks, his impatience growing
more palpable with each second.

His terse words are jumbled by his frustration.
"If—if—we do what you say—if we stop telling people to stand
when we sing or we can't say 'lame,' where does it end? Next
we'll be putting a parking space in the middle of the sanctuary
just because a disabled person asked for it!"

His huff intimates that this is the most absurd suggestion
ever. Five folks tore a roof off a house in Capernaum to get to
Jesus in Mark 2. I'm not sure offering accessible parking is the
worst outcome of asking my church to adopt more disability-
inclusive practices. Imagine if we began tearing roofs off houses
of worship to allow *everyone* access to Jesus. What a different
church that would be.

But I know this scriptural application won't make a difference
to this man, who had the audacity to come to this conference on
"ableism in the church" only to dismiss it as trivial because he's
never heard of ableism before now. "This isn't the gospel," he
definitively announces, "so we shouldn't get distracted. Where
does the Bible say we should care about disabled people?"

"Luke 14," I want to reply, but I know this question is rhetorical, with a side of sass. People often hide behind the slippery slope argument when asked to consider a perspective different from their own. The lurking fear of slippery slopes governs the public space. If this, then what? As though we'll descend into chaos if we are the least bit more inclusive. Everyone loves disabled people until we stop being inspirational and start asking for our access needs to be met. Inertia is easier to handle than inclusivity.

When I was younger, I thought slippery-slopers formed a coherent argument about how to implement accommodations. They'd blame cost or convenience or community as the reason we didn't include disabled people, and sometimes their concerns seemed legitimate to my teenage understanding of the world. "Where *would* we get the money?" I'd fret, not wondering why funds were never brought up when discussing a fancy Christmas tea or a summer camp for teens to play Kajabe Can Can.

Slippery-slopers would gnash their teeth over the slightest change for fear it would cause the house of cards to crumble. Whining over altering language. ("There are too many groups to keep up with nowadays.") Eye rolls at changing people's favorite songs with disability slurs. ("But we *love* that song! It's not meant to hurt anyone.") Stifled exchanges when refusing to put in a ramp, elevator, or parking space because they need to "steward tithe" well. As far as I could tell, "stewarding" was a way to make stinginess seem scriptural.

It might be worth noting that if your church service disintegrates when you cut out saying "lame" as a slur, you aren't worshiping God in the first place. If you're worried that spending money on a ramp or elevator isn't worth it, you probably aren't as welcoming to disabled people as you think. If you have concert lighting but don't have an accessible bathroom, you might have lost the plot of what church is a long time ago.

These excuses for not accommodating disabled people are contingent on absorbing the charity model of disability. In the charity model, we become objects of pity rather than subjects with our own gifts. Pity is far more condescending than its cousin, compassion, which seeks to meet people in their anguish and take it on *with* them. Pity feels sorry *for* someone, with little care for how to thwart future suffering. Pity is a duplicitous form of ableism because it dehumanizes the disabled person as an object of suffering, all while masquerading as a caring voice of support. It's the way that people's heads tilt and their voices raise to a pitch only dogs and dolphins can detect. It's their embarrassment over my body, as though they don't know where to look when I use my wheelchair or cane. Mobility devices are not the sun; you can look directly at them. It's the way they pat me on the head like I am a "good dog" and not a human being. Pity always reinforces a power structure between us because it keeps my accommodations contingent on your benevolence. It suggests that you oversee the guest list when it comes to the Lord's Table. This is not the model that Jesus describes when instructing us on how the kingdom of God functions.

"When you give a feast, invite the poor, the crippled, the lame, the blind," Jesus commands while eating at the house of a prominent Pharisee, "and you will be blessed, because they cannot repay you. For you will be repaid at the resurrection of the just" (Luke 14:13–14 ESV). Hearing this, one of the guests responds, "Blessed is *everyone* who will eat bread in the kingdom of God" (v. 15 ESV). Clearly the guest wants *his* banquet to be blessed. He shouldn't have to watch other people—people who proactively include poor and disabled neighbors—receive a blessing. He wants an IOU that promises to reimburse him for wining and dining with the elite.

Jesus is having none of it. He repeats, this time in parable form, "Go out quickly to the streets and lanes of the city, and bring in the poor and crippled and blind and lame," adding that "none" of the folks who refuse "shall taste my banquet" (14:21, 24 ESV). Jesus's message here is straightforward: include disabled and poor people. Seems simple enough.

Like other parables, this is a metaphor for what the kingdom of God is like. This particular parable is usually interpreted as eschatology, a branch of theology concerned with final judgments and new creation. We might say this is Jesus's description of what new creation is like. Disabled people are included "that my house may be filled" (14:23 ESV). Disabled folks are mentioned at this great banquet not as a form of pity or even as a precursor to curing their bodies. They are included to show who God invites to the table.

It's a metaphor, people are quick to assure me. Jesus doesn't mean disabled people, but folks who are *figuratively* in that category. "Aren't we *all* a little bit disabled?" Somehow my suggestion that we swap legs for a day isn't met with laughter. Snarky jokes aside, this response is exactly what Jesus corrects when the guest chimes in, thirsty for a blessing. This blessing, this repayment at the resurrection of the righteous, isn't for everyone. It's for those who welcome poor and disabled people.

When we erase disability from this narrative, we miss what Jesus tells us about the kingdom of God. Three out of the four of those mentioned are explicitly disabled, with the fourth category (poor people) often overlapping with disability, then as now. Jesus's invite list is not accidental or happenstance. Those of us who are disabled are not just tolerated, we are invited, sought out, and celebrated in the kingdom of God. To host "the crippled, the lame, and the blind," accommodations must be made. Ramps, communication aids, canes, comfy chairs— antiquity style. The great banquet is accessible! There is no "disability banquet" in a back room so folks aren't embarrassed by our access needs. There is no stifled exchange refusing to put in a ramp because they want to "steward tithe" well. There's no hand-wringing over whether they are attracting the wrong crowd. There is simply a host inviting poor and disabled people and receiving a blessing as a result. Yet again, disability comes with a blessing. Jesus doesn't need bouncers, preventing people from entering some exclusive feast. Jesus wants banqueters. Inclusive, poor, and disabled banqueters.

Folks who are "poor, crippled, blind, and lame" don't have anything to offer the host other than themselves. They are not influencers or celebs. They can't repay the host by reciprocating. They are simply wanted. They are enough. What's more, their attendance doesn't consume all the seats or food, because in kingdom economics, there is enough for everyone. Even after the poor and disabled guests are situated, the servant informs the host that "still there is room" at the table (Luke 14:22 ESV). Too often, slippery-slopers use cost and convenience to dodge accommodating disabled people's needs. That is not a part of Jesus's description of the kingdom of God. Cost is not a deterrent for including disabled people, at least not at Jesus's table. At the great banquet, poor and disabled people are accommodated first, and still there is room enough for everyone to partake. Like the remnant, if we build the banquet around disabled people, there will be enough space and yummy food for nondisabled people too. We don't need to make it a competition. Kingdom economics is not built on scarcity but abundance. There is enough for everyone at the table.

If for no other reason than to be repaid at the resurrection of the righteous, make space for disabled people at whatever table you are a part of. Jesus shuts down the idea that we must wait for a convenient time or calling to do this. The host instructs the servant to "go out quickly" to welcome disabled and poor people (14:21 ESV). Quickly. Go out quickly, Jesus commands. It is done with urgency because making room for poor and disabled people to belong is always timely. Yet including us takes intentionality and urgency.

Ask yourself, and be honest: Do you go out of your way, quickly, to include disabled and poor people? Have you provided accommodations for our access needs so we can dine at the table with everyone else? Have you focused on welcoming us, or acted more like a bouncer to an inaccessible table where exclusion is the main dish? Have you been a bouncer or a banqueter?

In many of our church spaces, we think it's on us to determine who is in and who is out. We spend a lot of time arguing over theological philosophies about the origins of disability instead of making space for more disabled people at the table. Let the slippery-slopers and disability doubters of each generation argue over who gets a seat at the table; we are going to keep setting out plates.

Jesus's description of the great banquet features poor and disabled people, much like the banquet Jesus's ancestor, David, hosts with Mephibosheth. At the height of his prestige, David seeks to bestow compassion on a remnant of Saul and Jonathan's family. The only problem? The lone remaining descendant is Mephibosheth, who is lame in both feet and a poor outcast as a result, because disabled people were not permitted to enter the palace (2 Sam. 5:8). Instead of dismissing him, David invites Mephibosheth to his table, which becomes a model for the kingdom of God in the prophetic imagination. David quells Mephibosheth's qualms over being summoned, reassuring him, "Do not be afraid, for I will show you kindness for the sake of your father Jonathan; I will restore to you all the land of your grandfather Saul, and you yourself shall eat at my table always" (2 Sam. 9:7). Always. Just as at Jesus's banquet, Mephibosheth is invited *always*.

Mephibosheth is not cured. He is simply welcomed, just as he is, to sit alongside the king and share a meal, "like one of the king's sons" (9:11). This is what the kingdom of God tastes like. It is not a tiny table with an exclusive guest list, accessible only to nondisabled elites, but an expansive one, where disabled and nondisabled people feast together, side by side, without animosity. It models what Ada María Isasi-Díaz calls a kin-dom, a space of mutuality and interdependence.[1] This banquet is accessible.

The narrative is intent on the audience remembering that Mephibosheth is disabled. We learn how he acquired his disability when he was five years old, even though this isn't particularly significant to the ongoing narrative. When news of Jonathan's and Saul's deaths reached Mephibosheth's nurse, she "picked him up and fled; and, in her haste to flee, it happened that he fell and became lame" (2 Sam. 4:4). Gives new meaning to blaming disability on "the fall." Mephibosheth's acquired disability is not glossed as sinful or in need of remedy; instead, what he needs is inclusive community. The banquet does not cure his lameness but offers a way to heal his isolation and ostracization.

To David, Mephibosheth is not a nameless exile who cannot enter his court; he is the son of David's beloved covenantal partner, Jonathan (1 Sam. 18:1–4). The way of keeping the covenant is to include disabled people—even those who are the grandson of your enemy—at the table. What's more, David restores Mephibosheth's land and position in society. Since Saul's other sons, Abinadab and Malchishua, also died fighting the Philistines at Mount Gilboa (1 Sam. 31:1–2), David restores Saul's inheritance to Mephibosheth to honor David's covenant with Jonathan and include Mephibosheth in a kinship network he would otherwise be excluded from because of his disability. Instead of treating him as a "dead dog," as Mephibosheth expects, David offers him financial and social support (2 Sam. 9:8). The narrative gives us an imagination

---

1. Ada María Isasi-Díaz, "Kin-dom of God: A Mujerista Proposal," in *In Our Own Voices: Latino/a Renditions of Theology*, ed. Benjamin Valentin (Maryknoll, NY: Orbis Books, 2010), 171–90.

for how disabled and nondisabled people can interact in the beloved community, and it starts with a nondisabled person extending an invitation and reparation to disabled people.

Just like the banquet that Jesus describes, this feast gives us a foretaste of the great banquet to come, like the most mouth-watering appetizer preparing us for the main meal. These banquets are mini representations of the kingdom of God. God does not ditch us to go to creation 2.0, plan B, the new and improved humanity software without any disability glitches. God redeems, restores, and rebuilds current creation with disabled people at the table. We, disabled and nondisabled people alike, get to join in the cocreation of new creation by setting the table for this accessible eschatological banquet. The church should be—and can be—like these banquets.

My hope is that one day, the slippery-sloper, prayerful perpetrator, and disability doubter can dine together at a banquet that centers "the poor, the crippled, the blind, and the lame," just as Jesus describes in Luke 14. That we limp, stim, roll, sign, and stroll to the accessible table set before us. When it comes to disability, churches have been too focused on causes and cures and not enough on community. Let's stop worrying about why I am disabled or how to make me *not* disabled, and instead let's focus on learning from my gifts as a disabled woman. Let's stop questioning whether disability is part of new creation and start curating crip spaces where we can flourish together. Let's stop baptizing our excuses in spiritual language and instead prepare a banquet where all access needs are accommodated without complaint. Let's rip the roofs off houses of worship so that all can get to Jesus.

I have experienced a foretaste of the banquet. Appetizers, you might say, for how new creation tastes. They are rare, but they are savored like my favorite dishes. Taste and see!

A group of friends sit in knowing silence as I share the details of my spoonie life. Joyful Resistance we call ourselves, because in one way or another, most of us know what it is like to be excluded from the main meal. Their faithful witness through dry humor and empowering GIFs has enlivened my imagination for what the kingdom can be. When I think of the remnant, I think of them. This is an appetizer for the banquet, like jalapeño poppers that ooze creamy white gold with each bite.

After I shared my experiences of ableism, two friends changed their own understanding of disability. Their receptiveness to learn reminds me that my wounds are valid and worthy of care. This is an appetizer for the banquet, like velvety potatoes wrapped in a crisp samosa and dipped in mint chutney.

"I'm sorry I caused a mosquito bite today," a pastor friend lamented after saying "lame" as a slur, before hurriedly changing the word. Her ability to realize and apologize soothed me. This is an appetizer for the banquet, like fluffy cheddar bay biscuits kissed with butter.

My friend started a book group for folks to learn more about disability in Scripture. The excitement to grow and equip others to do the same has been a gift I didn't know I needed. This is an appetizer for the banquet, like sweet, tangy pork cuddled in pillowy bao buns.

After learning the name of my mobility scooter, one of my friends bedazzled a Wonder Woman "W" for Diana to make her sparkle. Her joy celebrates my full, disabled self and accepts me as I am. This is an appetizer for the banquet, like zesty guacamole on just-fried tortilla chips glistening with salt crystals.

"Please leave the close parking space for Amy and park elsewhere," a friend texted a group of us heading to his house. The preemptive nature of his care reminds me I am not alone. This is an appetizer for the banquet, like sautéed brussels sprouts, post-'90s makeover when they began wearing balsamic vinegar.

My nieces and nephew race my scooter. They think my disability gadgets are fun and exciting, especially when I crank the speed from tortoise to hare. Their acceptance of my disability reminds me I am not a burden or a theological problem to those with childlike faith. This is an appetizer for the banquet, like gravy cascading down the flaky crust of an Aussie meat pie.

Dinner deliveries. Iced mocha surprises for long days full of medical appointments. Dog-walking shifts. Pasties and mint brownies. Wonder Woman GIFs. Bookmarks with *eshet chayil* (woman of valor) on them. Carpool shuttles to procedures. Flexible scheduling when I'm low on spoons. These appetizers prepare me for the main meal, reminding me that I have already experienced a dash of the divine that is to come. They cannot sustain me forever, but I relish them all the same. Most of these sprinkles of splendor require little money and few resources, but all demand intentionality and willingness to understand my full, disabled embodiment. None of them require awaiting the eschatological banquet for us to savor. We can feast now! We can cook up the banquet with our disabled neighbors, if only we are willing to taste it together. We can prepare a feast worthy of Jesus's description of the kingdom here and now.

Some of the friends included in this cloud of witnesses are the same people who unintentionally caused harm in other chapters. You will get it wrong sometimes. We all do. You will not realize something inadvertently excludes us until one of us fills you in. You will cause a mosquito bite or assume something on the basis of an expired vending machine choice. When someone courageously invites you into a more inclusive way, respond with grace. Listen, learn, and grow together. Focus on becoming a banqueter and not a bouncer. It might be awkward, and it will be messy, but it will be worth it.

And together we can taste the banquet, and it is delicious.

REFLECTION AND RESPONSE

▶ Reflect. How are you different after reading this book? What practices and ideas do you want to take with you into the world? What is the invitation for you and your community?

▶ Create a piece of art in any medium and style displaying the eschatological banquet from Luke 14, as discussed in this chapter. How can you include disabled body-minds without shame? How might this art inspire change in your own community? Post your art on social media with the hashtag #CripTheChurch and #MyBodyIsNotAPrayerRequest.

Accessibility note: Please make sure to capitalize the beginning of each word in the hashtag and offer an image description to make your post more accessible to people who use screen readers.

▶ Commit to change. What one item are you committing to change to make your sphere of influence more inclusive to disabled people? This can be related to language (become DEET!), access, or belonging. If you don't know what needs to change in your community, do your homework by listening to disabled people in and around your community. Don't wait for them to come to you. How can you encourage others to commit to change alongside you?

TOP TEN
Disability Dreams

These are my dreams for what church communities could become.

I dream that churches would . . .

10. Welcome change to become more inclusive and accessible to all disabled people.

9. Believe us when disabled people share that something is inaccessible to us.

8. Celebrate the holy disruption of disabled body-minds.

7. Incorporate disability theology into worship practices and gatherings.

6. Learn from the prophetic witness of disabled experiences.

5. Invite and equip disabled people to lead.

4. Budget money, time, and resources to make spaces and community etiquette more inclusive.

3. Create community care networks to support disabled people.

2. Pay the crip tax for disabled people in the community.

1. Worship the disabled God.

Bene*crip*tion
for Nondisabled People

I pray that this book has given you a broader perspective on disability. May you feel convicted to change what you can in your community. May you not rely on excuses or allow fear to prevent you from including disabled people at every opportunity. May you choose courage over cowardice.

I hope that you do the reading and refrain from weaponizing Scripture against disabled people. May you be prepared to listen to disabled people in your community, even when they tell you something you might not want to hear. May you be willing to change to be more like Jesus for the sake of the kingdom. May you name when you get it wrong, even unintentionally. May you not take yourself too seriously, and never be above critique. May you care more about the impact of your actions than the purity of your intentions. May you become a banqueter, not a bouncer.

I hope that you use the parts of my story that made you feel guilty as points of departure rather than destinations, knowing that there is always room to grow when grace abounds. May you never doubt that you are loved and cherished, even if you felt accused or called out by parts of my story.

May you have a deep sense of your worth that isn't dependent on equating yourself to others. May you avoid all comparison and hierarchy. May you learn to embrace your bodies and minds for what they can do instead of berating them for what they cannot. May your body-mind cease to be your adversary and become your trusted ally, and may you know deeply that it is a temple for the Holy Spirit. May you learn from the splendor of diversity in creation.

I hope my story has broadened your understanding of God. I pray that you don't dismiss or downplay the disabilities of Isaac, Jacob, Moses, Leah, Samson, Ehud, Mephibosheth, Zacchaeus, Paul, and Jesus, and that you learn from the gifts they can teach your community. May you extend your notion of what healing can be beyond physical forms. I pray that you learn to notice God's radiance in every disabled body, no matter how unpracticed you are with people who act and move and think and communicate in ways unlike your own. May you foster belonging instead of comfort, welcoming the holy disruption that disability brings.

May your community embody the banquet that Jesus describes in Luke 14. May you participate in the blessing of Jacob's disability every time you partake of the Lord's Table. May your love for God and for your disabled neighbors be deep enough to stretch you into the unknown. May it cast out your fears about getting it wrong, enabling you to trust that when you say the wrong word, miss an opportunity to be inclusive, or forget about disabled friends, you are beloved all the same. May your love be big enough to love anyway. May you foster belonging wherever you are, knowing that the prophetic witness of the disability community is worth the cost. May you learn from disabled people what it means to be human.

Benecription
for Disabled People

I hope that I have honored your experience. That you found in these words a glimpse of something you know to be true. I hope my story gives you one more way to help others understand ableism or disability or your life. I hope I reminded you that you are not alone. That even when no one gets it or you're the only one advocating for disabled people, you are not alone. I am in solidarity with you, and together we hope against hope that we can create the inclusive church that we have never fully experienced.

I pray that you follow Paul in boasting of your disability and learn the insights it gives you into God and incarnation and embodiment. I hope that you practice the trust of Moses to know that God is with your mouth, regardless of whether it speaks, and that God extends divine accommodations to you (as God did through Aaron). I hope you summon the courage of Jesus to display your redeeming scars to the world, knowing they reveal God's glory to us all, even the disability doubters and the prayerful perpetrators.

May you have a deep sense of your worth and value, even when those around you question it. May you have enough spoons for today and not fret about what will happen if you run out to-morrow, because you are surrounded by a community who will bring you endless casseroles without judgment or expectation of anything in return. May you never doubt that you are worth it. That no number of accommodations make it too costly or inconvenient to include you at the table. You are worth the cost.

May your story and disabled body teach the church what it means to bear God's image. May you never grow weary of valuing other disabled people. May you never act out of obligation or guilt, but from the love that casts out even our most pressing fears. May the deepest parts of you hope for something more inclusive, radically generous, and jubilant for all people, even the ones who just don't get it yet.

May you know who you are and not who they tell you to be. I pray that you know in the deepest part of your gut, and the loftiest neurons in your brain, that you are fearfully and wonderfully made. That your diagnosis doesn't take away from God's radiance that you display to the world. That God smiles upon you and declares you sanctified and redeemed. That you are cherished just as you are, crutches, chemical sensitivities, and all.

And on days when you are out of spoons or stamina for carrying the weight of everyone else's ableism, may the disabled God remind you that your disabled body is pure, holy, set free, capable, and meaningful to the kingdom. You are not a before picture in a prayer makeover or the symbol of sin used to guilt everyone into repenting. No, you, disabled friend, bear the image of the Creator of light, the Author and Perfecter of our faith, and the Alpha and the Omega. You are God's workmanship. You are made of the same stuff as the stars.

You are enough.

Acknowledgments

This book began with an email. My dear friend Cori Esperanza emailed me about a Global Writers Group that Freedom Road was launching and enthusiastically encouraged me to join. I didn't consider myself a writer or know whether I had anything to say, but a combination of my trust in Cori, her excitement, and my curiosity led me to check it out.

I am forever grateful for the sacred space I found in that group. Each Saturday morning, starting at 6 a.m., I met empowering, brilliant writers over video calls for four hours, in a space led by Lisa Sharon Harper, Chanté Griffin, Andre Henry, and Marlena Graves. There, in our dimly lit homes, across technology glitches, we shared our stories and dared to write a new world into existence. It is in that sacred space that I became a writer. To the people of that group: thank you for believing that I was a writer before I had the courage to admit it to myself. Your encouragement and creativity inspired and sustained me while I was writing this book. Special thanks to the leaders, Anna, Gigi, Sara, Alex, Olivia, Deborah, Ashley, Felicia, Amanda, Steve, Terri, and Grace for your kindness. It is a balm to hear your words each week.

Thank you to Lisa Sharon Harper for your prophetic witness and supportive presence. I am so grateful for the ways you invested in me and my writing. My heart is full from the fruitful conversations, accountability, and friendship that Chanté and Anna provided, writing with me every Tuesday and Thursday morning. Thank you to Ashley Abercrombie and Marlena Graves for recommending my work to Katelyn Beaty, and to Katelyn for being so kind, astute, and all-around easy to work with. Eric Salo, Erin Smith, and the entire team at Brazos have been wonderful, and I am so appreciative.

Before I joined the group, Meisha Battiste suggested I embrace my disability community, Emily Maynard helped me process all the things, and Nish Weiseth was a constant source of refuge and rejuvenation throughout. I appreciate their sage advice. To the people who generously read or listened to chapters and offered gracious feedback—Sara, Anna, Cori, Nick, Ashly, Mason, Lacey, Dawn, Ren, Debbie, Brenna, Erin, Ruth, my parents, Dave, Jordo, and Liss—I cherish your time and support as I brought this book into the world. Thank you for every cheer and critique; this book is the better for it. Thanks to Bella for being a great book buddy!

This book was written during the global pandemic, when life, work, and physical therapies were relocated to the glorious 531-square-foot space I share with my husband and husky. While I was writing it, we were evacuated from our home due to California wildfires, and I endured various medical surprises, including one three weeks before the book was due. I wrote passages on my phone in hospital waiting rooms, on napkins in the car while traveling to the doctor, and in the sacred space of my bed when it hurt too much to leave.

I am thankful for my body, and for the land that I currently live on, which was home to the Tongva people before me. I am so grateful to be surrounded by a community of friends and (chosen) family who have nourished my soul and life in ways too numerous to recount here. I think of this book less as the thoughts of a single person and more as a result of the wonderful and wacky communities that I am honored to have called my own. If you have been a part of any of these communities, I thank you for the role you played, even if you are not mentioned here by name.

Thank you to my in-laws for letting us stay with them when we were evacuated, and to them and my parents for all the prayers, pasties, mint brownies, and abundant meals that served as writing fuel. I am grateful for the encouragement and giggly happy hours with Liss, and for my family for believing in me even when I doubted myself.

Thank you to Paul for the inspiring art, to Nancy for the stimulating reading material, to Mary for the hilarious affirmations, and to all our friends at Hart Park for showing me the beloved community so well. Best wishes and warmest regards to Original Lady Assassins for always curating space for me to be my full self. I treasure both of you. I cannot thank Joyful Resistance enough for being the faithful remnant with endless casseroles. I am grateful for the prophetic questioning of Mason; the erudite encouragement of Ren; and the quiet courage of Dr. Debbie. Thank you to Dawn for being the constant and radiant lighthouse who shines such discerning and loving guidance in my life; to Ruth for being a cherished disability ally, coparent, and costar in our own *Lifetime* movie; and to both of you for being willing to learn and grow alongside me. Thank you to Cori for believing in me more than I believed in myself, for doing the hard work of allyship, and for cheering me on through tulips and jalapeños. I am a little more like Jesus from having known each of you.

To my fellow spoonie, Lacey, thank you for getting it—*all* of it—and reminding me that my pain is real and worthy of care. I am not as alone because of you. We, with our rare bodies and resilient spirits, are fireproof.

And all my gratitude to Andrew, who by now has heard me wrestle with each idea and phrase of this book, giving wise advice and motivating me with iced mochas, green Post-it notes, and reassuring words, even before 6 a.m. every Saturday. I wouldn't have the courage to share my story without you. Thank you for believing I am extraordinary. The truth is, together, we create something magical. You might even call it jubilee.

Further Reading

Eiesland, Nancy. *The Disabled God: Toward a Liberatory Theology of Disability*. Nashville: Abingdon, 1994.

Fox, Bethany McKinney. *Disability and the Way of Jesus: Holistic Healing in the Gospels and the Church*. Downers Grove, IL: IVP Academic, 2019.

Hardwick, Lamar. *Disability and the Church: A Vision for Diversity and Inclusion*. Downers Grove, IL: InterVarsity, 2021.

Hull, John M. *In the Beginning There Was Darkness*. Harrisburg, PA: Trinity Press International, 2002.

Nielsen, Kim. *A Disability History of the United States*. Boston: Beacon, 2013.

Reynolds, Thomas E. *Vulnerable Communion: A Theology of Disability and Hospitality*. Grand Rapids: Brazos, 2008.

Samuels, Ellen. "Six Ways of Looking at Crip Time." *Disability Studies* 37, no. 3 (2017). https://dsq-sds.org/article/view /5824/4684.

Sins Invalid. *Skin, Tooth, and Bone: The Basis of Our Movement Is Our People; A Disability Justice Primer.* 2nd ed. Berkeley: Sins Invalid, 2019.

Swinton, John. *Becoming Friends of Time.* Waco: Baylor University Press, 2018.

Tait, Stephanie. *The View from Rock Bottom.* Eugene, OR: Harvest House, 2019.

Wong, Alice, ed. *Disability Visibility: First-Person Stories from the Twenty-First Century.* New York: Vintage, 2020.

Yong, Amos. *The Bible, Disability, and the Church: A New Vision of the People of God.* Grand Rapids: Eerdmans, 2011.

VISIT AMY-KENNY.COM TO ACCESS THE

DISABILITY JUSTICE HUB

FOR REFLECTIONS, QUIZZES, ART, AND MORE!

AMY-KENNY.COM